PRE-ELECTION POLLING

Sources of Accuracy and Error

PRE-ELECTION POLLING
Sources of Accuracy and Error

Irving Crespi

RUSSELL SAGE FOUNDATION / NEW YORK

The Russell Sage Foundation

The Russell Sage Foundation, one of the oldest of America's general purpose foundations, was established in 1907 by Mrs. Margaret Olivia Sage for "the improvement of social and living conditions in the United States." The Foundation seeks to fulfill this mandate by fostering the development and dissemination of knowledge about the political, social, and economic problems of America. It conducts research in the social sciences and public policy, and publishes books and pamphlets that derive from this research.

The Board of Trustees is responsible for oversight and the general policies of the Foundation, while administrative direction of the program and staff is vested in the President, assisted by the officers and staff. The President bears final responsibility for the decision to publish a manuscript as a Russell Sage Foundation book. In reaching a judgment on the competence, accuracy, and objectivity of each study, the President is advised by the staff and selected expert readers. The conclusions and interpretations in Russell Sage Foundation publications are those of the authors and not of the Foundation, its Trustees, or its staff. Publication by the Foundation, therefore, does not imply endorsement of the contents of the study.

Library of Congress Cataloging-in-Publication Data

Crespi, Irving.
  Pre-election polling : sources of accuracy and error / Irving
Crespi.
    p.   cm.
  Bibliography: p.
  Includes index.
  ISBN 0-87154-208-0 (alk. paper) :
  1. Public opinion polls.   I. Title.
  HM261.C68 1988
  303.3'8—dc 19

88-15770
CIP

The paper used in this publication meets the minimum requirements of American National Standard for Information Sciences—Permanence of Paper for Printed Library Materials, ANSI Z39.48-1984.

10 9 8 7 6 5 4 3 2 1

Acknowledgments

Without the financial support provided by the National Science Foundation and the Russell Sage Foundation, it would have been impossible to conduct the research upon which this report is based. The research design included both a quantitative and a qualitative phase. The National Science Foundation's funding of the quantitative phase (under Grant No. SES 8318145) made it possible to develop an extensive data base for the statistical analysis of the correlates of accuracy in pre-election polling. The National Science Foundation does not bear any responsibility for the data analyses or any of the conclusions drawn from them. The Russell Sage Foundation's funding of the qualitative phase, which involved lengthy personal interviews with leading poll practitioners, added a body of information that could not have been obtained in the quantitative phase, which provided a depth of understanding to many of the issues raised in the quantitative phase.

The Bureau of Social Science Research provided essential organizational support to the conduct of the quantitative phase. Thanks are due especially to Albert Cantril for making the bureau's facilities available and for his continuing encouragement.

Charles Roll, Jr., provided invaluable assistance in translating a disparate body of information on the results of individual pre-election polls into a form that made them usable for quantitative analysis. The statistical guidance and advice provided by David Cantor of the Bureau of Social Science Research added immeasur-

ably to the analysis of the quantitative data. David Naden of the Bureau of Social Science Research directed the data entry and tabulation aspects of the quantitative study.

The compilation of pre-election polls for the quantitative phase was greatly facilitated by an anonymous organization that provided access to its file of newspaper clippings on public opinion polls and by Warren Mitofsky, who provided a list of state polls that he had developed for the CBS News Election and Survey Unit.

A special debt of gratitude is due to Susan Cantril for her assiduous shepherding of all phases of the quantitative phase of the study. Somehow she always managed to keep all the strands of activity under control.

A final expression of gratitude is also due to Paul Perry, from whom I learned so much about pre-election polling over two decades of professional association.

IRVING CRESPI

Contents

List of Tables

PRE-ELECTION POLLING
Sources of Accuracy and Error

1 /  Introduction

The failure of the public opinion polls to predict correctly the outcome of the 1948 presidential elections created wide confusion and misgivings about the reliability of the polls. Reaction of the public to the polls ranged from charges of outright fraud to expressions of personal sympathy for the pollers. Reactions of experts ranged from condemnation for carelessness, unintentional bias, errors of judgment, and use of outmoded techniques, to a determination to make use of this experience to enlarge our knowledge of political behavior and to improve survey methodology. After an initial period of shock and embarrassment, the main reaction of the pollers was to initiate objective studies to find out what went wrong.

So wrote S. S. Wilks in the opening chapter of the report of the Social Science Research Council (SSRC) on the performance of the 1948 pre-election polls (quoted in Mosteller et al. 1949, 1). The intervening years have seen many changes in poll methodology, for example, in sample design, treatment of turnout, interviewing methods, and timing. To varying degrees, these changes have resulted in improved accuracy. For example, the average deviation from election results of the Gallup Poll has been reduced from

3.6 percentage points in eight national elections from 1936 to 1950 to 1.2 percentage points in seven national elections from 1972 to 1984 (*Gallup Report* 1986).

Nonetheless, after two decades in which some of the leading national pre-election polls compiled an enviable accuracy record, in the early 1980s professional pollsters became increasingly concerned about inaccurate polls. According to Warren Mitofsky, director of the CBS News Election and Survey Unit, the performance of pre-election polls during the 1980 presidential election campaign raised doubts among some observers about the capabilities of many pollsters and the methods they use. After reviewing poll performance in the 1982 elections, Burns Roper, president of The Roper Organization, asserted that there was "a consistent failure in the opinion polls. Almost without exception, the indicated front-runner in the polls fared worse than the polls said he would." Roper concluded, "We have a problem" (1983). In response to a suggestion by Roper, a session entitled "Performance of the Polls in the 1982 Elections: What Have We Learned" was added to the program for the May 1983 national conference of the American Association for Public Opinion Research (AAPOR) specifically to discuss 1982 pre-election polls that differed markedly from actual election outcomes. Commenting on the disagreement among polls as to the magnitude of Reagan's 1984 victory, pollster Irwin Harrison told the *Wall Street Journal*, "There's no science in the questions. There's no science in the interviews. And there's more art than science in the results." Roper expressed a similar attitude: "I'm very concerned. This raises real questions of whether this business is anywhere near a science" (*Wall Street Journal*, 8 November 1984, 7) (see also Field 1981).

The reasons for this unease about pre-election polling accuracy are obvious from a brief review of some of the more publicized errors in recent years. One poll conducted prior to the 1977 New York Democratic mayoralty primary had the three leading candidates ranked in the reverse order of actual voting (though it should be noted that the deviations were within sampling error). In 1978, a number of polls seriously misread the political situation in key senatorial elections. Polls conducted just prior to the 1980 New York Democratic presidential primary were far off the mark. As for the 1980 presidential election, just about every poll under-

estimated Reagan's strength, leading to the widespread conclusion that the race was "too close to call"; in fact, Reagan defeated Carter by a comfortable margin. In 1982, the winning margins projected by polls in the Illinois and California gubernatorial elections were substantially in error, while the Texas gubernatorial election was an unheralded upset. A poll conducted days before the 1983 Chicago mayoralty primary ranked the three candidates for the Democratic nomination incorrectly, with the winning candidate a poor third in the poll, and a poll conducted just prior to the 1983 Philadelphia Democratic mayoralty primary correctly called the winner, but with a large percentage point error.

In 1984, all polls correctly projected that Reagan would win by a comfortable margin, with the Gallup Poll's 59%–41% corresponding exactly with the actual election results. However, there was considerable variation among polls as to the magnitude of Reagan's victory, from an underestimate of 55%–45% by Roper to an overestimate of 60%–35% (with 5% undecided) in the poll conducted by Gordon Black for *USA Today*.

What is particularly disturbing about these deviations of pre-election polls from election results is that they have not been confined to new, inexperienced polling organizations. Organizations with previously good accuracy records have also had large errors. For example, four survey companies—Gallup, Market Facts, Market Shares, and Richard Day Research—which differ considerably in polling experience—conducted polls for the news media prior to the 1982 Illinois gubernatorial election. All reported results that were within sampling error of each other but overestimated Thompson's margin of victory by a wide margin (Day 1983).

An evaluation of pre-election polling as practiced in the 1980s is clearly in order. This report presents the results of a study designed for that purpose. Although conducted in the spirit of the SSRC evaluation of the 1948 polls, this study takes a very different approach. The SSRC study sought to explain what went wrong with the polls in one presidential election by analyzing in detail the methods and performance of a limited number of organizations that conducted polls prior to that election. In comparison, this study is based on a review of the variety of methods used by numerous polls in a large number of different types of elections

for the purpose of identifying the correlates of poll accuracy. Instead of identifying the limitations of poll methodology that would explain a particular polling error, therefore, this study seeks to identify the sources of variability in the accuracy of polling.

PRE-ELECTION POLLS AS PREDICTIONS

Interest in pre-election polls has always been based on the expectation that they can provide accurate advance indications of election outcomes. Nonetheless, since 1948 professional pollsters have repeatedly asserted that their results should be considered measures of voting preferences as they were at the time a poll was taken and that intervening events can, and on occasion do, significantly change voter preferences subsequent to the end of interviewing. Thus, a vexing question in any evaluation of the methods employed to measure voting intentions is: In what sense, if any, can those measures be considered predictions? Only after this question has been answered can we speak with clarity about poll accuracy and inaccuracy.

To begin, we must distinguish between how accurately polls measure voting preferences as they exist at a given time and how accurately those preferences predict what people do on election day. The fact is that predicting an election on the basis of a pre-election poll always involves, implicitly even if not explicitly, a *projection* from the interviewing dates to election day. Conceivably, a pre-election poll could be a highly accurate measurement of voting intentions at the time it was taken and still deviate significantly from the election outcome. Since that is the case, how can one use election results to evaluate the predictive accuracy of a pre-election poll? For example, if a September poll deviates appreciably from a November election, it is fruitless to analyze that deviation in an attempt to evaluate its methodology. Conversely, it would be incorrect to treat a September poll that corresponded closely to election results as if it were an accurate prediction of the election outcome.

Even though a pre-election poll is in itself unquestionably a

measurement and not a prediction, concluding that even if a poll were conducted immediately before an election, one cannot hope to measure voter preferences accurately enough to approximate election results closely is to impugn the meaningfulness of all polls. If polls cannot achieve such accurate predictability, why should we accept any poll results as having meaning relevant to real life? In fact, using the deviation of pre-election polls conducted close to election day from election results as a measure of accuracy does provide an objective criterion when evaluating alternative methodologies for measuring voting preferences. It is only in this specific sense, and for this specific purpose, that the concept of poll accuracy is used in this study.

Furthermore, confidence in the accuracy of polls of voting preferences conducted sometime before an election as measures of then existing preferences is bolstered if methods that have been tested in polls conducted immediately before elections have been used (even if those early preferences correlate poorly with subsequent behavior). For example, two polling organizations measured voting preferences in the 1986 Missouri senatorial election about six weeks before the election, with sharply conflicting results. One had the Republican and Democratic candidates running "neck and neck" (with a sampling error margin of +/− 3.7 points), while the other showed the Republican candidate leading by 14 percentage points (with a sampling error margin of 4.9 percentage points) (William Robbins, "Two Skillful and Tireless Foes Battle in Missouri Senate Race," *New York Times*, 1 October 1986, B9). Comparing the results of these two organizations' polls conducted just prior to the election with the election results would provide an empirical basis for judging which of the earlier polls is more likely to have provided an accurate measurement of voter preference in September.

With the above observations and provisos in mind, for this study pre-election poll accuracy is defined as the closeness in percentage points of voting preferences to election results. To allow for change in preferences, only the last polls reported before election day are considered, and the time gap between interviewing for those polls and election dates is analyzed as a correlate of accuracy.

THE SIGNIFICANCE OF POLL ACCURACY

The significance of poll accuracy goes far beyond the credibility of commercial polls. If contemporary pre-election polls are providing inaccurate measures of voting intentions, the implications for all research on voting behavior need to be assessed. Valid analyses of the correlates of voting behavior based on surveys conducted before an election (as distinct from election day exit polls) are contingent on having accurate measures of voting preferences. Voting preferences are widely used in analyses of how adherents for competing candidates differ in their perception of those candidates, in their issue orientation, their party identification, their psychological characteristics, and their group memberships and identifications. The validity of such analyses obviously depends on the accuracy with which voting intentions are measured. Determining what contributes to or explains inaccuracy in commercial pre-election polls can, therefore, contribute to the design and analysis of voting behavior research.

The accuracy of pre-election polls is also of interest because polls offer a natural setting for testing the relation between verbal expressions of attitude and behavior. Rosenberg and Hovland's conceptualization of attitudes as having a behavioral component (including statements of how one will act in a given situation) in addition to a cognitive and an affective component (1960, 4) applies here. That voting behavior can be predicted accurately on the basis of pre-election polls would tend to support those who contend that attitudes are predictive of behavior. Conversely, pre-election poll inaccuracy would lend support to those who claim that the power to predict behavior on the basis of verbalized attitudes has yet to be satisfactorily demonstrated.

Finally, it should be remembered that the excellent accuracy records of some polling organizations in national elections during the 1960s and 1970s have obscured the fact that large polling errors in pre-primary polls are not new. A review of the poor accuracy record of pre-primary polls conducted in the 1950s and 1960s concluded that "it seems unlikely that pre-primary polls will ever be able to accrue an accuracy record comparable to that of pre-election polls" (Mendelsohn and Crespi 1970, 119). It should, therefore, not come as a surprise that a number of the polling

errors cited above involved pre-primary polls. However, since other inaccurate polls covered state and local elections, one must wonder whether the accuracy of state and local pre-election polls is subject to the same sources of error that have always plagued pre-primary polls. Also, polling errors in the 1980 and 1984 presidential pre-election polls raise the question of whether pre-election polls in all general elections, and not only those conducted in state and local contests, are becoming subject to those sources of error. Although this study is not designed to answer that question, by examining the relation of political context to polling accuracy it does provide some information bearing on the issue.

STATE AND LOCAL POLLS

The current ubiquity of pre-election polls, especially in state and local elections, has considerably enhanced their methodological significance for election research. Albert Gollin of the Newspaper Advertising Bureau reports that at a 1982 meeting of the Newspaper Research Council representatives of over 100 newspapers indicated that they conduct polls. In addition, CBS News identified about 150 state pre-election polls conducted in 1980 (personal conversations). Instead of evaluating election poll methodology only on the basis of the performance of a limited number of polling organizations in national elections, we now can also examine the accuracy records for the many polls conducted each year prior to state and local elections.

The availability of pre-election polls at the state and local levels has a further significance, if their accuracy can be verified. The study of voting behavior at these levels has been the object of increasing attention, and research in this important area would be enhanced if the methodological problems in accurately measuring state and local voting intentions were to be resolved.

INADEQUATE POLLING LITERATURE

One barrier to a proper assessment of the accuracy of pre-election polls is the lack of information about their actual perfor-

ance, their methodologies, and why their methods may or may not be satisfactory. Gallup is unique even among the major national polls in that it has regularly published its complete national accuracy record in presidential and congressional elections since 1936, when it conducted its first pre-election poll. As for the many state and local polls noted above, no effort has been made to compile their accuracy records. Thus, despite the attention given to polling errors by the news media, very little is known about the overall accuracy record of pre-election polls. It is true that the news media often publish overviews of poll performance immediately after an election, especially if there are notable errors (see, for example, *New York Times,* 20 October 1984, 8). The usefulness of these overviews is limited by their narrow coverage, the fact that they have never been gathered into a single compilation, their anecdotal treatment of why errors occur, and their neglect of methodological issues that are of primary concern to survey researchers (Converse and Traugott 1987). As a result, media reports are too hit-or-miss for meaningful conclusions to be drawn from them as to the extent of the accuracy of pre-election polls and what factors correlate with accuracy.

Apart from media reports, there have been few attempts since the SSRC investigation of the 1948 pre-election polls to evaluate pre-election poll methodology. Charles Roll (1968) restricted his analysis to the performance of the street-corner straw polls conducted by one newspaper. A review I compiled (Mendelsohn and Crespi 1970) was limited to pre-primary polls in presidential years, although I did include a discussion of what might account for conflicting poll results. A pioneer effort to compile and evaluate the accuracy of national polls (Hennessy and Hennessy 1961) is flawed in two ways: (1) it used as its accuracy criterion whether or not a poll correctly "called" the election regardless of the poll's percentage point deviation from the election, and (2) the time interval between interviewing dates and election day was ignored. In 1984, Adler reviewed methodological differences between major national pre-election polls that might account for variations in their estimates of the Reagan-Mondale election but did not include state and local elections or pre-primary polls. More recently, Buchanan reviewed the accuracy of national pre-election polls in the United States and overseas to assess how closely they conformed

to theoretical estimates of sampling error, but he did not relate accuracy to methodology (1986).

Although there is a sizable literature on political polling, most of it deals with its political functions and influence on policy making (e.g., Gollin 1980; Bogart 1972; Sudman 1982; Cantril 1980; Roll and Cantril 1972) rather than on poll methodology and accuracy. Most commercial pollsters have published little or nothing on their methods. The outstanding exception is Paul Perry's series of articles describing Gallup's methods (1960, 1962, 1965, 1973, 1979). To some degree, the failure of pollsters to develop a methodological literature can undoubtedly be ascribed to a desire to protect competitive commercial interests. But, judging from the cooperation received from pollsters in the course of this study and the openness of discussions at annual meetings of AAPOR, lack of interest in creating a literature and lack of time in which to do it appear to be even more important.

The large academic literature on voting behavior does little to compensate for the failure of commercial pollsters to develop a methodological literature. The academic work has typically focused on identifying and analyzing the determinants of voter decisions and voting behavior rather than on the methodological problems encountered in measuring voting intentions. A recent illustration is an analysis of turnout (one of the most important measurement issues in pre-election polling) by Raymond Wolfinger and Steven Rosenstone (1980), which examined why voting participation has declined, in which the methodological problem of how to differentiate voters from nonvoters received secondary attention. While John Katosh and Michael Traugott analyzed the tendency for more people to report that they are registered to vote and have voted than is actually the case (1981), they did not consider the implications of their analysis with respect to the accuracy of voting intentions as measured in pre-election surveys. Stanley Kelley, Jr., does present a method for measuring voting preferences based on open-ended questions that might be a usable alternative to the structured "trial heat" questions typically used by pollsters, but with the purpose of interpreting the political meaning of election results rather than predicting election outcome (1983).

In recent years, there has been some progress in developing a

methodological literature specific to the problems encountered in pre-election polling, as distinct from the extensive general literature on survey methodology. Illustrative of this are a number of papers describing experience in the design and conduct of pre-election polls, for example, how to allocate "undecided" voters (Fenwick et al. 1982), how to identify likely voters (Traugott and Tucker 1984), the effects of call-backs on the political representativeness of samples (Traugott 1987), and the effect of question order on the measurement of candidate preference (Crespi and Morris 1984).

This study contributes to the growing literature on the methodological issues involved in pre-election polling by not only determining what the accuracy record of pre-election polls has been, but also by seeking to identify the methodological correlates of accuracy in those polls. An additional distinguishing characteristic of this study is its scope and depth. Unlike most previous investigations that have concentrated on national presidential elections, this study also encompasses polls related to elections for state and local offices and to primaries as well as general elections. It is also concerned with the relation of methodology to political context. Finally, it analyzes how what pollsters say and think contributes to accuracy, and it empirically tests their beliefs.

2 / Design and Conduct of the Research

RESEARCH OBJECTIVES

This study investigates and evaluates the correlates of accuracy of media-sponsored pre-election polls in state and local as well as national elections. The study focuses on media-sponsored pre-election polls for two reasons: (1) the results of media polls are in the public domain, unlike most "private polls" conducted for candidates and parties, and therefore are relatively accessible; and (2) media polls are designed to measure voting preferences and, unlike private polls, are not primarily intended to provide guidance for campaigning that is meant to change preferences. That is, many private pollsters are more interested in guiding campaign directors than in obtaining precise measurements of candidate strength (personal conversations). Despite the focus on media-sponsored polls, the goal of this investigation is to evaluate pre-election poll methodology in order to contribute to the scientific study of voting behavior rather than to the accuracy of commercial polls.

The study's central tasks were to (1) assess the extent of poll accuracy (and inaccuracy); (2) to identify the correlates of accuracy; (3) to investigate the capabilities and limitations of current

state-of-the-art polling; and (4) to assess the reasons for existing limitations. The methodological issues involved in relating measured voting intentions as they exist at a given time to subsequent voting behavior are analyzed in this context. This analysis, it is hoped, will make it possible to identify potentially fruitful lines of research designed to analyze the process whereby voting intentions are translated into voting behavior.

Although this is a methodological study, I anticipate that it will also contribute to theoretical studies of voting behavior. For example, identifying likely sources of measurement error in pre-election polls should help in any analysis of changes in voter volatility from election to election. Similarly, analyses of the stages of voter decision making in any one election would be furthered by improvements in methods for measuring voting preferences.

In order to assess the accuracy of pre-election polling, two types of issues need to be addressed, those related to methodology and those related to the political environment. While chairing the session on the 1982 polls held during the May 1983 conference of AAPOR, Everret Ladd speculated that What was wrong with the polls? might not be the proper question to ask. Instead, he suggested that recent accuracy problems may be inherent in the phenomenon—that today's electorate may be more difficult to study than was the electorate of years past and that we do not know enough to study it properly (notes taken at the session). This comment sets up a crucial opposition of views concerning the sources of poll inaccuracy.

At one extreme are those who see faulty or inadequate methodology as the source of error. For them, when pre-election polls are in error it is because not enough effort has been invested in the development and application of sound methodology, for example, commonly used identifiers of likely voters and ways of treating undecided voters are ineffective. Usually associated with this view is the belief that a standard methodology equally usable in any and all elections is an achievable goal. At the other extreme are those who point to volatility, commitment, partisanship, and "hidden issues" as influences on voting behavior that change from election to election and that, consequently, can lead to poll error even when previously accurate methods are used. Implicit in

this view, though not always articulated, is the belief that different methods may be required in different elections in order to cope with their idiosyncrasies.

A complete methodological assessment of pre-election polls must deal with both kinds of issues, namely: (1) the methods used by pre-election polls to measure voting intentions, and (2) the relation of those methods to the political environment in which they are used. Furthermore, it is necessary to evaluate intermediate perspectives that see merit in considering both measurement issues as such and the effect of changing political environments on polling accuracy. This study examines polling experience in relation to both sets of issues.

Two sets of data were collected:

1. A qualitative survey: personal interviews with leading pollsters on their experiences in polling and the methodological lessons they have drawn from those experiences.

2. A quantitative survey: a compilation of media-sponsored pre-election polls, respective election results, the political context of the elections covered by those polls, and the methodologies of the polling organizations that conducted them.

The Qualitative Survey X

The qualitative survey centered on compiling and evaluating the largely unpublished "professional lore" of pollsters as it relates to the accuracy of pre-election polls. *Professional lore* refers to what pollsters believe they have learned with respect to measuring voter preferences accurately. These lessons have usually been learned "the hard way," that is, through cut-and-try "experimentation," subjective assessments as to what happened in various elections, and, sometimes, rigorous testing. No assumption is made regarding the correctness of this professional lore. In fact, since there is disagreement among pollsters on a number of issues, some of the lore is bound to be incorrect. Nonetheless, compiling and evaluating it is of value, for two reasons. First, some part is based on tested, though unpublished, experience. Second, knowledge of this lore is essential to an understanding of the practices that now characterize pre-election polling and, therefore,

to an understanding of what accounts for poll accuracy—or lack thereof.

This phase of the research is based on extended, informal interviews with practicing pollsters concerning the methodological principles and practices that guide their pre-election polling. All of the interviews were conducted by the principal investigator, mostly in person but in a few instances by telephone. The personal interviews took about two to three hours each, while the telephone interviews lasted about one to one and a half hours. In most cases, the pollster and the principal investigator had known each other professionally for many years, and in the remaining instances we were at least professionally aware of each other. Thus, the interviews had more of the flavor of a conversation between colleagues on matters of professional interest than that of a research activity by an anonymous stranger. This contributed substantially to the productivity of the interviews. In a number of instances, the interviews were supplemented by correspondence and other written materials.

The interviews were conducted as semistructured conversations. Instead of following a prescribed protocol, they touched on a varying assortment of topics depending on the interests and concerns of the pollster. On occasion, and as appropriate, references were made to issues and perspectives that had been raised by other pollsters. As a result, not every topic was covered in every interview, and some topics were probed more intensively in some interviews than in others. The advantage of this procedure is that each pollster talked primarily about those methodological issues that were of most concern to him and about which he had the most to say. In this way, the interviews brought to the fore the full range of methodological concerns that are salient to pollsters without imposing an a priori conceptual framework. The consequent inability to quantify the interviews is not a drawback since such an analysis had never been contemplated.

The interviews were analyzed first to identify the methodological issues that pollsters believe must be considered in any evaluation of pre-election poll accuracy and the range of options that they saw as available to them in trying to cope with those issues. The results of this analysis were used to guide the development of a questionnaire for the quantitative survey; in this respect, the

qualitative survey served as a pilot for the quantitative phase of the study.

The interviews were also analyzed to identify issues on which there appears to be a consensus or, if not that, a convergence of thinking among pollsters. When that occurred, they were further analyzed to determine, if at all possible, the underlying bases for consensus and/or convergence. Similarly, whenever there was disagreement among pollsters, the interviews were reviewed in an effort to specify the sources of conflict. The results of these analyses were then related to the findings of the quantitative survey in order to (1) test quantitatively the professional lore of pollsters, and (2) add a quantitative dimension to the conclusions that can be drawn from the interviews.

Only individuals active in the conduct of pre-election polls were interviewed. One criterion for selection was that in addition to the major national polling organizations, pollsters that conduct only state and local pre-election polls should be represented. A second criterion derives from the fact that state pre-election polls are conducted not only by commercial survey firms but also by academically based pollsters. Since practices might differ between the two, both are represented. A final consideration was that although this study focuses on media-sponsored polls, talking with some pollsters who conduct private polls would also be informative. The most feasible way to satisfy these criteria was to select a purposive sample of pollsters.

Of the thirty-one pollsters who were contacted, only one declined to be interviewed, on the grounds that his methods are proprietary. Of the thirty who agreed to be interviewed, none raised this issue; in fact, they were very cooperative and appeared open in describing their methodologies. One indication of the cooperative attitude is that, on their own initiative, some of the pollsters provided copies of questionnaires and internal memos. Also, the larger organizations arranged for more than one person to be present at the interview, so that all questions could be answered immediately.

The persons interviewed, and the organizations they represent, are listed below. When more than one person was present at the same interview, they are listed on the same line. When separate interviews were conducted with individuals representing the

same poll, they are listed on different lines. Interviews that were conducted by telephone are asterisked. It should be noted that most of the national organizations conduct state polls as well.

I. National polling organizations
    A. ABC News/*Washington Post* Poll
        1. American Broadcasting Company:
            Jeffrey Alderman, John Brennan
        2. *Washington Post:* Barry Sussman, Kenneth John
        3. Chilton Research (ABC subsidiary): Dan Hagan*
    B. CBS News/*New York Times* Poll
        1. CBS News: Warren Mitofsky
        2. *New York Times:* Adam Clymer
    C. NBC News Poll: Roy Wetzel, Laurily Epstein
    D. The Gallup Organization:
        Andrew Kohut, Diane Colasanto
        Paul Perry (retired)
    E. Louis Harris and Associates:
        Humphrey Taylor, David Neft
    F. The Roper Organization: Burns Roper
    G. *Los Angeles Times* Poll: Irwin Lewis
    H. Gordon S. Black Corp. (*USA Today* Poll): Gordon Black
II. State polling organizations
    A. The California Poll: Mervin Field, Mark DiCamillo
    B. *Chicago Sun Times* Poll: William Brady
    C. *Chicago Tribune* Poll: John Timberlake, Russell Brooker
    D. Rocky Mountain Poll: Earl deBerge
    E. *New York Daily News* Poll: Richard Link
    F. Market Shares Corporation: Nick Panagakis
    G. R/L Associates: Michael Rappeport
    H. The Iowa Poll: Glenn Roberts*
    I. Teichner Associates: Steve Teichner*
III. Academically based pollsters
    A. Stephen Cole, State University of New York at Stony Brook
    B. G. Donald Ferree, University of Connecticut, Storrs
    C. F. Chris Garcia, University of New Mexico
    D. Bruce Merrill, University of Arizona, Tempe
    E. Philip Meyer,* University of North Carolina, Chapel Hill
    F. Michael Traugott, University of Michigan
    G. Alfred Tuchfarber, Robert Oldendick,
        University of Cincinnati
    H. Cliff Zukin, The Eagleton Institute, Rutgers University
IV. Private pollsters
    A. Peter Hart,* Peter D. Hart Research Associates
        (Democratic)
    B. Robert Teeter, Market-Opinion Research Company
        (Republican)

Finally, James E. Dannemiller of SMS Research, which polls for the *Honolulu Advertiser*, sent a letter describing some of the methods his organization uses.

The Quantitative Survey

In the quantitative survey, we complemented and extended the data obtained in the qualitative phase by compiling reports on the results of pre-election polls, obtaining information about the methodologies employed in conducting those polls, and ascertaining key characteristics of the elections themselves. These data were analyzed to (1) develop a measure of the accuracy of the pre-election polls, individually and in the aggregate; (2) determine the extent to which the polls share a common methodology and measure the range of methodological differentiation among them; (3) measure the extent to which methodological differences are associated with variation in poll accuracy; and (4) measure the extent to which differences in the political environment are associated with variation in poll accuracy.

Two time restrictions were placed on the compilation of pre-election polls. One was to consider only "final" polls, final in the sense that if more than one poll was conducted on a race only the last one would be considered and in no event would "trial heats" conducted before nominations were made be included. This restriction conforms to the understanding of poll accuracy previously described. Second, only polls conducted subsequent to 1979 were included. Initially, it had been planned also to compile polls conducted during 1970–72, so that a comparison of two time periods could be made. However, it rapidly became clear that news media could not be expected to search that far back in their files for both methodological procedures and poll results, so it was necessary to confine the search to pre-election polls conducted during the later period only.

Developing a frame for sampling pre-election polls presents some formidable problems. Defining the population of national survey organizations that conduct pre-election polls is simple since there are a limited number of media-sponsored and media-conducted pre-election polls at the national level. All of them were included with certainty in the survey. The situation is quite differ-

ent with respect to the myriad pre-election polls sponsored by local news media. The sheer volume of those polls, the diversity of local newspapers and television stations that sponsor them, the diversity of facilities used to conduct the polls, and differences in when local election days are scheduled make locating such polls a cumbersome and complicated task.

Three separate lines of inquiry were used to locate pre-election polls. One was to construct a list of survey organizations known or believed to conduct pre-election polls, based primarily on the membership of the National Council on Public Polls and the Network of State Polls. Letters were sent to each asking them to provide releases or reports on the results of all final pre-election polls they have conducted during the specified time period. Second, Mitofsky made available a list of news media that have sponsored state pre-election polls in past years. Letters were sent to each asking them for releases or reports on their polls. Third, an organization that has requested that its identity not be divulged provided access to a news clipping file it maintains on public opinion polls. This proved to be a particularly useful source. We also explored the possibility of using the files of wire services to locate news reports of pre-election polls but found that such files are not maintained.

These three lines of inquiry located final pre-election polls on 446 separate races, and, as described below, usable information was obtained for 430 of them. (If voter preferences were measured for more than one race in a particular election, each measurement is counted as a separate poll.) These polls comprise the basis for the quantitative phase of the study, with no further sampling. It is reasonable to assume that they make up a large proportion of all media-sponsored pre-election polls conducted during the specified time period, even though the total cannot be considered exhaustive, nor can these be considered a probability sample of media-sponsored pre-election polls conducted during the specified time period. Nonetheless, they do constitute a sizable and extensive data base that includes the major types of media-sponsored pre-election polls. As such, they are an appropriate base for this study.

An alternative procedure would have been to use published lists of newspapers and television stations as a frame for developing a probability sample of local media. That sample could then

and primary elections, and respondents were asked to reply for each type. Information was requested regarding interviewing method; interviewing hours; whether demographic quotas are assigned and, if so, what kind; whether all voting-age adults, only registered voters, or only likely voters are interviewed; respondent selection procedure; treatment of not-at-homes; treatment of refusals; whether the sample is weighted and, if so, for what characteristics; use of ratio or regression adjustments; treatment of "undecided" responses; methods for dealing with turnout; household selection procedures; use of stratified and cluster sample designs; position of candidate preference question in questionnaire; length of interview; and whether questions unrelated to the election were asked in the interview.

Three questions were also asked regarding organizational structure—who designs and analyzes the pre-election polls, the type of interviewing staff, and the importance of accurate prediction of elections when evaluating the success of the pre-election polls. A final question asked for a description of recent changes in methodology. A copy of the questionnaire appears as an appendix.

As appropriate, these methodology questionnaires were sent directly to the polling organization or to the sponsoring news media with a request that they be completed by "the person most familiar with the methods used to conduct your pre-election polls." Many of the sponsoring media and polling organizations had conducted more than one poll, so it would have been excessively burdensome to ask that a separate questionnaire be completed for each poll. Instead, each organization was asked to complete one questionnaire, which was then linked to each poll that organization had conducted. A total of 125 questionnaires [were] mailed. In some cases, these overlapped in that a question[naire] was mailed both to a sponsoring medium and to an outside [surve]y organization that actually conducted its polls. A total of 66 [of thes]e questionnaires were linked to 343 individual national, [...] and local polls (methodological information was not ob[tained] for 87 polls) covering a variety of offices, including the [preside]ncy, and both primary and general elections. Tables 2.1, [and] 2.3 describe the types of elections that were covered by [34]3 polls.

TABLE 2.1 / OFFICES AT STAKE

Office at Stake	All Polls (%)	Accuracy Tercile		
		High (%)	Medium (%)	Low (%)
President	28	29	34	21
Senator	21	24	18	23
Governor	14	12	13	16
Other state offices	12	15	11	11
Congressman	12	9	12	12
County official	3	3	3	5
Mayor	2	4	1	2
Other local office	†	1	—	—
Referendum	6	3	8	7
Other	2	1	1	4
Total	100	102*	99*	99*
Number of polls	(430)	(139)	(139)	(139)

*Total does not add up to 100% because of rounding.
†Less than 1%.

TABLE 2.2 / GEOGRAPHIC COVERAGE OF POLLS

Geographic Area	All Polls (%)	Accuracy Tercile		
		High (%)	Medium (%)	Low (%)
Statewide	74	77	72	72
Congressional district	11	9	14	11
County	8	5	9	12
Municipality	3	4	2	2
National	3	4	4	1
Other	1	1	—	2
Total	100	100	101*	100
Number of polls	(430)	(139)	(139)	(139)

*Total is more than 100% because of rounding.

ALTERNATIVE MEASURES OF POLL ACCURACY

Earlier, we defined accuracy as "the closeness in percentage points of voting intentions to election results." That definition

TABLE 2.3 / TYPE OF ELECTION

Type of Election	All Polls (%)	Accuracy Tercile		
		High (%)	Medium (%)	Low (%)
General election	73	78	73	70
Primary	23	20	21	27
Referendum	3	2	6	3
Total	99*	100	100	100
Number of polls	(430)	(139)	(139)	(139)

*Total is less than 100% because of rounding.

leaves unanswered the question of how to calculate the percentage point deviation between pre-election poll results and election returns. Complicating this question is the fact that many polling organizations report their results including the percent undecided. Since there is no undecided vote in the election booth, to maintain comparability it is necessary to do something about the undecided. One standard procedure is to calculate the poll results excluding the undecided. This procedure in effect assumes that the undecided do not vote and/or split proportionately as do the decided. Another procedure is to allocate the undecided evenly between the major candidates. Since the former assumption comes closest to the experience of most pollsters who were interviewed in the qualitative survey (some referred to unpublished, in-house analyses that support this assumption), it was adopted.

Three alternative ways of calculating the deviation of poll results from election returns (after allocating the undecided) were tested:

1. The difference, in percentage points, between the percentage the winning candidate received in the election and what he or she received in the final poll, disregarding sign.

2. The mean percentage point difference between the election and the poll for the top three candidates, considering only those candidates who received at least 15% of the vote in the election, again disregarding sign.

3. Considering the same group as in Method 2, the largest percentage point difference between the poll result for each candidate and his or her percentage of the actual vote (see Table 2.4).

have been surveyed to determine which sponsored pre-election polls during the specified time period. This approach, however, would have been inefficient and unproductive since, despite the increase in the number of pre-election polls conducted each year, a relatively small proportion of local media sponsor them.

The releases or published reports for each pre-election poll were scanned to obtain the following information:

1. Geographic coverage: national, state, county, municipality, congressional district

2. Date of the election

3. Type of election: general, referendum, Democratic primary, Republican primary

4. Office at stake

5. Size of sample

6. Interviewing dates

7. Poll results: the percentage for each candidate and the percentage undecided

8. Interviewing method

These data were supplemented by two additional bits of information—the official election results, including the number of votes cast for each candidate and the total vote cast in the election, and the total voting-age population for the geographic area sampled by the poll. For most of the polls, election results were obtained from the appropriate issue of *America Votes*, though in a number of instances it was necessary to contact state or county election officials. These data were used to calculate (1) the actual percentage of votes for each candidate with which the poll data could be compared, and (2) the turnout rate for each election. A file of complete information was compiled for 430 pre-election polls.

To obtain more detailed information about the methodologies used to administer the polls, a mail survey of the sponsoring news media and/or polling organization was conducted. This questionnaire asked for ". . . the standard method now used to conduct your pre-election polls. If your methods differ when conducting final pre-election polls as compared with earlier polls, please describe the final pre-election poll methodology only." Space was provided to describe methods separately for national, state, local,

TABLE 2.4 / COMPARISON OF THREE METHODS
FOR CALCULATING POLL ERROR

	Method 1	Method 2	Method 3
Mean error	5.67	5.68	6.75
S.D.	4.69	4.32	5.10
Minimum error	.01	.03	.03
Maximum error	29.50	29.50	33.25
Number of cases	(343)	(343)	(343)

The three measures produce very similar results. The correlation between Methods 1 and 2 is .89; between Methods 1 and 3 it is .81; and between Methods 2 and 3 it is .93. Clearly, the three measures are virtually interchangeable. Since Method 1 is the simplest, it was used in preference to the others.

Analysis plan. Two types of analyses were used, cross-tabulation and regression. Poll accuracy was used as the dependent variable in both types.

For univariate cross-tabulations, it was possible to categorize 423 of the 430 polls into high-, medium-, and low-accuracy terciles, each with an *n* of 141, as follows:

1. High accuracy: polls with a deviation from election results of 3.05 points or fewer. The mean error is 1.55, with a standard deviation of .88, and the median error is 1.65.

2. Medium accuracy: polls with a deviation between 3.05 and 6.36 points. The mean error is 4.6, with a standard deviation of .98, and the median error is 4.67.

3. Low accuracy: polls with a deviation of 6.40 points or more (the maximum recorded error is 29.5 points). The mean error is 10.86, with a standard deviation of 4.38, and the median error is 9.42.

The independent variables in the cross-tabulation analyses were the methodological and political environment characteristics obtained from poll releases and the methodological questionnaires. The key statistic in each case is the percentage of all polls with specified characteristics that is in the high-accuracy tercile, for example, the percentage of polls based on quota and nonquota samples respectively that are in the high-accuracy tercile. Using this statistic focuses attention on the extent to which each independent variable is associated with a high order of accuracy.

Although the quantitative survey is not based on a probability sample, tests of significance were performed for their heuristic value. For this, the standard error of the difference in the percentage of polls in the high-accuracy tercile was calculated for pairs of characteristics. Differences outside the confidence band at the 95-in-100 confidence level are treated as significant.

For the regression analyses, the actual deviation in percentage points for each poll was the dependent variable. The selection of independent variables to include in the regression model was constrained by the nature of the data obtained from the methodological questionnaire. It will be remembered that this questionnaire asked about the standard poll methodology used by each organization and that this information was then linked to all the polls conducted by each one. Thus, the same bit of methodological information was linked to varying numbers of polls. This means that any correlation between methodological characteristics taken from that questionnaire and accuracy could be confounded by what may be called a house effect, that is, the existence of some general characteristic of each polling organization. The validity of the regression analysis would, of course, be severely compromised by such an effect. For this reason, the independent variables in the regression analyses were limited to those obtained from the poll releases plus a surrogate for the house effect taken from the methodological questionnaires, namely, expressed importance of accuracy as a goal in pre-election polling.

It is evident that the regression analyses did not examine the combined contributions to accuracy of the independent variables measured in the methodological questionnaire. As a partial substitute for regression analysis of the data from the methodology questionnaire, an additional series of cross-tabulations were performed. For these, a matrix based on selected pairs of independent variables was constructed and the mean error calculated for all polls within each cell. The significance of differences between cell means was tested by a t test.

THE MAGNITUDE OF ERROR IN PRE-ELECTION POLLS

Using the definition of polling error adopted for this study—the difference in percentage points between a poll's measure of the

winning candidate's share of voter preference (after excluding the undecided from the percentage base) and his or her share of the actual vote—the mean error for the 430 polls compiled for the quantitative survey for which data are available is 5.7 points. The mean sample size used in those polls is 756.

How likely is it that a mean error of that size would occur through chance alone? To test the null hypothesis that the mean error of 5.7 points is attributable to sampling error, instead of using the usual standard error of a percentage we have used the theoretical *average* error of a percentage. We have done so because our purpose is to test the likelihood that the mean error of the 430 polls will occur through chance. That is, we want to compare an observed mean error with the theoretical mean error for a series with a specified average sample size. Therefore, instead of asking What is the standard error of the distribution of the 430 polling errors? we ask What is the theoretical variability expectation of the mean error of the 430 polls given their average sample size of 756?

The average error for a normally distributed variable is $(.7979 \ldots) \times (\sigma)$. Thus, assuming a 50-50 split, the theoretical average error for a series of simple random samples with an average size of 756 is about 1.7 points. A reasonable allowance for increased variance in cluster samples would increase the average error by about 25%, that is, to about 2.1 points. Since the polls compiled for this study were based on both unclustered and clustered samples, we can estimate that the expected average error lies between 1.7 and 2.1 points. That is, the actual mean error of 5.7 points is roughly three to four times as large as what would be expected through chance alone.[1]

Clearly, pre-election polls are subject to appreciable nonsampling error. The task of our analysis is to identify and, to the extent possible, to quantify the nonsampling sources of error in pre-election polls.

---

[1] By way of comparison, William Buchanan's assessment of the accuracy of pre-election polls, in which he compared the standard error of the average percentage of the total vote obtained by winning parties with the theoretical standard error for his estimate of average sample size, led him to conclude that the "standard deviations of the errors for winning parties turns out to be . . . twice what would be expected" (1986). His analysis was based on national elections, while ours is based largely on state and local elections and primaries. As we shall see, polls on state and national elections and on primaries have a poorer accuracy record than do polls on national elections. Taking all these differences into account, Buchanan's assessment is comparable to ours.

3 / Sampling

PROBABILITY VERSUS NONPROBABILITY SAMPLING

Controversy between adherents of probability and nonprobability sampling was central in the Social Science Research Council's evaluation of the 1948 pre-election polls. Although the sampling procedures used by pollsters have changed in many ways since then, this issue persists. Some pollsters are now committed to probability designs, while many others use designs that include probability procedures at some but not at all stages of sample selection. Thus, most pollsters who use quotas also incorporate probability procedures in such stages as the selection of primary sampling units, block clusters, and households (e.g., in random digit dialing). As a result, many of the more egregious sources of sample bias that characterized quota samples used by pollsters in the 1940s do not appear in most current nonprobability samples.

Many of the pollsters personally interviewed are not concerned that the use of nonprobability methods may be a significant source of error for their polls. Illustrative of this perspective is Teeter's comment that his "problem" polls did not have a sampling problem—though they did have "design" problems. Garcia was initially committed to probability sampling but has now concluded

TABLE 3.1 / THE USE OF DEMOGRAPHIC QUOTAS

	All Polls (%)	Accuracy Tercile		
		High (%)	Medium (%)	Low (%)
Use of Quotas				
Yes	46	45	48	47
No	54	55	52	53
Total	100	100	100	100
Number of polls	(353)	(118)	(122)	(104)
Type of quota used				
Sex	42	40	43	43
Race/ethnicity	18	20	16	16
Age	7	13	6	4
Geographic	5	5	6	5
All other	14	19	11	12
Total*	86	97	82	80
Number of polls	(353)	(118)	(122)	(104)

*Totals are greater than the percentage that use quotas because of multiple responses.

that at the operational level there is little to choose between pre-election polls that utilize costly, full-scale probability samples and those that employ samples that within a general probability structure deviate at the final stages of selection. Even Mitofsky, who is sharply critical of deviations from probability designs by many pollsters, added that a "sloppy probability design can be worse than a quota sample."

Of the polls in the quantitative survey, 46% were conducted by organizations that use at least one type of quota in their pre-election polls (see Table 3.1). There is no difference in the accuracy of polls conducted by those who do not use quotas and those who do: 33% of the former and 36% of the latter are in the top tercile of poll accuracy (see Table 3.2). This does not argue that quota samples are inherently as accurate as probability samples.

It should be noted that some pollsters who do not use quotas also do not use random procedures for selecting respondents within contacted households. Thus, a nonquota sample is not necessarily a probability sample. Another consideration is that, as noted above, among those who do use quotas, probability

TABLE 3.2 / ACCURACY AND THE USE OF QUOTAS

Accuracy Tercile	Quota Not Used (%)	Quota Used (%)	Type of Quota Used			
			Sex (%)	Age (%)	Race/ Ethnicity (%)	Geographic (%)	Other (%)

Accuracy Tercile	Quota Not Used (%)	Quota Used (%)	Sex (%)	Age (%)	Race/Ethnicity (%)	Geographic (%)	Other (%)
High	33	36	32	58	40	33	46
Medium	37	34	37	27	32	39	28
Low	30	30	31	15	28	28	26
Total	100	100	100	100	100	100	100
Number of polls	(161)	(183)	(145)	(26)	(60)	(18)	(50)

methods are employed at many stages of selection, with quotas applied most often after probability methods have been used to select households, primarily to achieve a "correct" sex ratio in the obtained sample. That is, quota sampling is largely restricted to sex, in contrast to the previous practice of assigning multicriteria quotas (for example, sex quotas in combination with age and with socioeconomic status): 42% of the polls had a sex quota, while the next most commonly used quota characteristic, race, was employed in 18% of the polls. Age quotas are applied to only 7%, and none reported using an education or income quota. Moreover, many of the pollsters who use only a sex quota do so in connection with a respondent selection procedure (described later in this chapter) that excludes, or at least severely restricts, interviewer judgment. As will also be noted below, sample weighting adds to the accuracy of polls that employ quota samples. Furthermore, as we shall see, some telephone probability samples are compromised by high refusal rates and inadequate call-back schedules. Everything considered, though, it is apparent that accuracy depends on more than the avoidance of quota sampling.

In this context, it is pertinent to note that many of the pollsters personally interviewed emphasized that ultimately what is needed in pre-election polling is a sample of voters—or "likely voters"—and not a general population sample. This need is discussed in detail in Chapter 4 as a separate problem. But, as is implicit in a variety of comments in the personal interviews, it is considered by pollsters to be as significant for accuracy as is sampling. For example, in discussing British experience, which reportedly has been that quota samples have been more accurate than probability samples, Mitofsky commented that the former are drawn from registration lists while the latter are of the total voting-age population. He believes that failure to identify likely voters adequately when using probability designs to sample the total population accounts for the poor performance of British probability samples. (The problem of identifying likely voters is partially solved when registration lists are sampled, even if by quota). Similarly, Field argues that most differences between competing pre-election polls derive not from differences in sampling but from the way the electorate is "modeled"—that is, how the various polling organizations go about identifying likely voters.

TELEPHONE SAMPLES

Almost all pre-election polling is now conducted by telephone. Fully 98% of the polls in the quantitative survey were so conducted. Of the national polling organizations, only Gallup and Roper still use personal interviews for their pre-election polling. The widespread adoption of telephone interviewing in pre-election polling has furthered the use of probability methods in the selection of households since it is easier, and less expensive, to draw a sample of telephone households than it is to draw a sample of all households. As Clymer points out, one reason probability telephone samples have become common in polling is that they appear deceptively easy to design and implement. But, he continues, "This can seduce you into thinking the problems are solved."

The practice of sampling telephone numbers from telephone directories has virtually disappeared (see Table 3.3). The switch to some form of random digit dialing results from an awareness of and a concern about unlisted and out-of-date numbers. Of the

TABLE 3.3 / SELECTING TELEPHONE SAMPLES

| | | Accuracy Tercile | | |
Selection Procedure	All Polls (%)	High (%)	Medium (%)	Low (%)
Computer generated random numbers	69	64	73	71
Select sample of numbers from directory and generate numbers to call from them	17	23	15	14
Sample registration lists and get telephone numbers of those selected	4	4	2	6
Select sample of numbers to call from telephone directory	1	—	1	—
Other	7	4	7	9
Don't conduct telephone interviews	2	5	2	—
Total	100	100	100	100
Number of polls	(353)	(118)	(122)	(104)

TABLE 3.4 / ACCURACY AND GENERATING TELEPHONE
              NUMBERS

	Method for Generating Numbers	
Accuracy Tercile	Computer-Generated (%)	Generated from "Seed" Numbers (%)
High	32	45
Medium	37	30
Low	31	25
Total	100	100
Number of polls	(238)	(60)

polls in the quantitative survey, 1% were drawn from directories. When telephone directories are used to draw samples for polls, it is to obtain "seed" numbers from which to generate the numbers to call rather than to select households, for example, by adding a random number to the last digit or pair of digits in the selected number: 17% of the polls in the quantitative survey were based on this type of sample.

Some type of computer-generated random digit dialing is the dominant design, with 69% of the polls in the quantitative survey conducted by organizations that use computer-generated numbers. Despite the theoretical superiority of computer generation, 32% of the polls that used this method are in the high-accuracy tercile, compared with 45% of those in which telephone directories were sampled to obtain seed numbers (see Table 3.4).

While random digit dialing has solved many of the problems in drawing telephone samples for pre-election polls, other problems remain. According to a number of pollsters who were personally interviewed, one problem that has sometimes introduced a serious bias, especially in state and local elections, is the underrepresentation of minorities in telephone samples. For example, Merrill notes that in states like Arizona in which about half the population is Hispanic or Indian, many members of which groups do not have telephones, obtaining proper representation in a telephone sample is very difficult. Black has found that getting a good sample of minorities is a problem in central cities, though not in the suburbs. In one Cleveland poll that he conducted, blacks con-

stituted only 28% of his telephone sample rather than the 45% that the makeup of the city would have prescribed. He suspects that multihousehold use of a single telephone may be one reason for this bias. If he is correct, bias resulting from the exclusion of non-telephone households, especially in low-income and minority areas, may be greater than is usually realized. Field counters that members of nontelephone minority households tend to be non-voters, so that minority underrepresentation is less a problem when measuring the preferences of likely voters than might other-wise be the case. In any event, even with random digit dialing, special measures apparently need to be taken to ensure proper minority representation in telephone polls. This undoubtedly ac-counts for the relatively high incidence of the race or ethnicity quotas noted above.

A problem that arises when polling by telephone on congres-sional, county, and municipal elections is creating a satisfactory frame for sampling. Telephone-exchange boundaries typically do not coincide with political boundaries, and reconciling the two in telephone surveys can be very difficult—some say impossible—when random digit dialing is used. Even if the initial selection of seed numbers is limited to numbers that can be identified from their addresses as being within the polling area, there is no way of telling where the generated numbers will be located. Also, poll-sters have found that respondents are a poor source of informa-tion regarding the congressional district in which they live. One solution is to give up the advantages of random digit dialing and sample from reverse listings in which telephone numbers are or-dered by street address. (Survey Sampling, Inc., a firm that a number of pollsters use as a source for their telephone samples, reports that it can draw samples for congressional districts based on listed numbers.) However, in some urban areas sampling only listed numbers results in excluding over one-fourth of the resident population, clearly a sizable bias.

THE EVALUATION OF SAMPLE ADEQUACY
AND SAMPLE WEIGHTING

Two perspectives regarding the evaluation of sample adequacy differentiate pollsters. One, typified by Mitofsky, examines de-

signs in terms of rigorous adherence to the principles of probability sampling; for example, when creating an appropriate frame, it would use known probabilities at every stage of selection and would employ call-backs to achieve maximum completion rates. The other focuses not on the design as such but on the "representativeness" of the obtained sample.

Pollsters like Mitofsky do not ignore sample composition when evaluating samples, and they do weight their samples to adjust for deviations from known population parameters. However, their goal is to eliminate bias and control variance and not merely to create a "representative" sample. In accordance with sampling theory, Mitofsky uses weighting variables as part of an a priori estimating model. For that purpose, he has identified significant correlates of the dependent variable—in this case, voting preference—so that controlling (weighting) for them reduces the variance of the dependent variable. This approach emphasizes the elementary principle that sample efficiency is enhanced by weighting only if the weighting variables are sufficiently correlated with voting preference and that this can and should be determined independently of the composition of any given sample. It contrasts with atheoretical *post hoc* efforts to create the appearance of a representative sample when an obtained sample deviates from population parameters.

Among the pollsters who emphasize representativeness when evaluating their samples are some who use probability designs as well as those who use nonprobability samples. The primary concern of this group of pollsters, regardless of whether they use probability designs, is whether the demographic profiles of their obtained samples correspond well with known parameters. Since the function of weighting, from their perspective, is to obtain a representative sample, their decision to weight is *ad hoc*. Thus, Field weights "only if adjustments are needed," and Taylor weights "to correct any bias in the obtained sample."

In sharp contrast are pollsters like Timberlake who prefer not to weight at all. Timberlake's position is that large weighting factors add to variance, while small factors make no difference in poll results. Pollsters who do weight their samples also expressed concern that large weighting factors can increase variance. For this reason, they typically restrict weighting to the minimum they feel is necessary. Mitofsky's observation that only variables with a

demonstrated ability to reduce variance should be used is obviously relevant here. Pollsters who weight their samples answer critics like Timberlake by citing the contributions this practice has made to poll accuracy. Meyer, for example, determined in a post-election analysis that if he had weighted a 1984 North Carolina sample by age and race, his error would have been only 1 point instead of 5.3 points in the Reagan-Carter race, 1.1 points instead of 5.1 in the Helms-Hunt race (senatorial), and 1.6 points instead of 2.6 in the Martin-Edmisten (attorney general) race.

Turning to the quantitative survey, 32% of the polls were conducted by organizations that weight their pre-election polls as part of their standard practice, 35% were conducted by pollsters who weight as necessary, and 33% were conducted by pollsters who never weight (see Table 3.5). Polls conducted by organizations

TABLE 3.5 / SAMPLE WEIGHTING

		Accuracy Tercile		
	All Polls (%)	High (%)	Medium (%)	Low (%)
Weights Sample				
Yes, as standard procedure	32	41	27	30
Yes, if necessary	35	39	37	30
Does not weight	33	20	36	40
Total	100	100	100	100
Number of polls	(348)	(117)	(120)	(102)
Weighting factors used by those who weight				
Sex	62	61	61	64
Age	58	59	59	56
Race/ethnicity	52	50	48	61
Political party identification	41	40	49	33
Education	26	27	19	34
Geography	19	18	19	20
Size of household	14	3	19	26
Other	28	30	24	31
Total*	300	288	298	325
Number of polls	(233)	(94)	(75)	(61)

*Totals are greater than the percentage that weight because of multiple responses.

TABLE 3.6 / ACCURACY AND WEIGHTING

		Weights Sample		
Accuracy Tercile	Total (%)	Standard Procedure (%)	If Necessary (%)	Never Weights (%)
High	41	44	38	22
Medium	33	29	37	40
Low	26	27	25	38
Total	100	100	100	100
Number of polls	(232)	(110)	(122)	(107)

that do not weight their samples are significantly less likely to be accurate than are polls conducted by those that do weight: 22% of the former are in the high-accuracy tercile as compared with 38% of those that weight when necessary and 44% of those that weight as part of their standard procedure (see Table 3.6). The difference between polls conducted by those who weight only as needed and those conducted by those who weight as part of their standard procedure is not statistically significant.

The lack of a statistically significant difference between the two approaches to weighting warrants consideration. Many pollsters who weight only if necessary to adjust for discrepancies in their obtained samples are sensitive to the fact that weighting variables differ in their utility. Lewis, for example, has evaluated the effect of different weighting variables to determine which "do something," that is, which result in a change in measured voting preference. Thus, the actual practices of pollsters who say they weight on an *ad hoc* basis often differ little from those who establish a priori weighting models. Both weight by similar variables when there are sizable sample discrepancies, the former after a poll-by-poll assessment and the latter because it is part of their standardized weighting model. One condition under which the results of their practice will differ is when the obtained sample varies from known parameters that do not correlate strongly with the dependent variable.

It is noteworthy that weighting tends to increase the accuracy of both quota and nonquota samples (see Table 3.7). The average

TABLE 3.7 / ACCURACY, WEIGHTING, AND QUOTA SAMPLING

	Combined Use of Weighting and Quota				
	Weights Sample	Quota Used	Mean Error	S.D.	*n*
a.	Yes	No	5.12	4.68	102
b.	No	No	6.21	4.22	46
c.	No	Sex only	7.92	5.77	22
d.	Yes	Sex only	5.21	4.41	53
	a vs. b	$t = 1.38$	$\alpha = .10$		
	c vs. d	$t = 1.48$	$\alpha = .10$		
	d vs. b	$t = 1.14$	not significant		

a = Yes/No; that is, weights and doesn't use quota.
b = No/No; that is, doesn't weight and doesn't use quota.
c = No/Sex only; that is, doesn't weight and uses only a sex quota.
d = Yes/Sex only; that is, weights and uses only a sex quota.

error of samples with sex quotas is 7.9 points when unweighted and 5.2 points when weighted. Similarly, the average error of unweighted nonquota samples is 6.2 points, compared with 5.1 points among weighted nonquota samples. Both of these differences are significant at the .9 confidence level.

Despite this evidence of the contribution that weighting makes to poll accuracy, a cautionary note of Sussman's is pertinent. In the 1981 Virginia gubernatorial election, his and another poll had similar demographic profiles but differed in their candidate standings. Sussman believes that the reason for this is that although women were equally represented in the two polls, they differed in their internal demographics, leading to a difference in the measured voting preference of women. It was not sufficient only to have women represented in their correct weight in the two samples; it was also necessary to have a good sample of women. This experience underscores the often overlooked principle that demographic quotas do not protect against sample bias within demographic groups. Furthermore, weighting is useful as a fine-tuning procedure and not as a substitute for good sample design.

Garcia expressed doubts about weighting, but for reasons different from Timberlake's. Garcia's doubts relate to the fact that it is

the voting population and not the total voting-age population whose preferences are pertinent in pre-election polls. His experience in New Mexico state polls is that, normally, sample biases parallel variations in voting turnout; that is, underrepresented population segments are normally those characterized by low turnout. Garcia believes that even if his samples are biased with respect to the total voting-age population, they are unbiased with respect to the voting electorate. He, therefore, points to the danger that weighting an obtained sample by total population parameters may result in a biased sample of actual voters.

As Garcia's comments indicate, pollsters who weight their samples have to cope with the questions of what population base to use when constructing their weighting model and how to obtain the appropriate weighting factors for that population. Many pollsters interview only registered voters (40% of the polls in the quantitative survey) or only those they identify as likely voters (20% of the polls in the quantitative survey)—without obtaining demographic data for those screened out (see Table 3.8). Pollsters

TABLE 3.8 / POPULATION INTERVIEWED

	All Polls (%)	Accuracy Tercile		
Sample Population		High (%)	Medium (%)	Low (%)
Registered voters only; screen out nonregistered	40	52	34	33
Likely voters only; screen out unlikely voters	20	12	25	21
All voting-age adults for entire questionnaire	16	15	18	14
Registered voters for entire questionnaire, plus nonregistered for demographics	10	6	11	16
Likely voters for entire questionnaire, plus unlikely voters for demographics	10	10	10	8
Other	1	1	—	3
More than one method	3	4	2	5
Total	100	100	100	100
Number of polls	(353)	(118)	(122)	(104)

do this primarily for cost reasons, though they also justify the practice by saying there is no purpose in interviewing those who clearly will not vote. Census data on the total voting-age population are, by definition, not appropriate for weighting such samples.

While some pollsters, like Garcia, conclude that it is therefore not advisable to weight their samples, a number use other sources to estimate weighting factors. Panagakis uses exit poll data from past elections, supplemented by data from recent polls, to estimate weighting factors. However, exit poll data are often not available, limiting severely the practicality of this procedure. Black feels that despite the systematic overestimation in census data of the proportion registered, census data on the demographic characteristics of registered voters, compared with total population data, are sufficiently reliable to use for calculating weighting factors. At this time, there is no evidence to establish the merits of these various alternatives, though census estimates of the demographic characteristics of registered voters, if they have been recently updated, would appear to be the most satisfactory.

In theory, the optimum solution would seem to be the practice of many other pollsters who interview all voting-age adults and filter out unlikely voters at the analysis stage (16% of the polls in the quantitative survey) or who screen out likely nonvoters only after obtaining basic demographic data for them (10% of the polls in the quantitative survey) (see Table 3.8). When either of these procedures is followed, census data can be used as weight parameters. In either case, the presumption is that filtering out likely nonvoters after weighting will produce a proper sample of likely voters. However, the proportion of polls in the high-accuracy tercile conducted by organizations that follow these procedures is not consistently higher than the percentage conducted by organizations that do not (see Table 3.9).

There was wide agreement among the pollsters who were personally interviewed that sex, age, and race or ethnicity are basic characteristics that should be used as weighting factors (see Table 3.5). In the quantitative survey, 62% of all the polls were conducted by organizations that weight by sex. This compares with 68% of all the polls conducted by organizations that use at least one weighting factor. In other words, virtually all the organiza-

TABLE 3.9 / ACCURACY AND POPULATION INTERVIEWED

Accuracy Tercile	All Voting-Age Adults (%)	Registered Voters for Entire Questionnaire; Nonregistered for Demographics (%)	Registered Voters Only; Nonregistered Voters Screened Out (%)	Likely Voters for Entire Questionnaire; Others for Demographics (%)	Likely Voters Only; Others Screened Out (%)
High	33	19	44	38	21
Medium	40	35	31	38	46
Low	27	46	25	25	33
Total	100	100	100	101*	100
Number of polls	(55)	(37)	(137)	(32)	(67)

*Total is more than 100% because of rounding.

tions that weight their polls use sex as a weighting factor. Age, race, and political party identification also figure prominently as weighting factors: 58% weight by age, 52% by race, and 41% by political party. Less common are education (26%), household size (14%), income (1%), and a variety of other characteristics (28%). The proportion of polls in the high-accuracy tercile is almost identical regardless of which weighting variables are used. This is not surprising since, as just noted, if any weighting is performed, it almost never is done unless sex is one of the variables used. On the basis of the data available from the quantitative survey, it is impossible to measure any independent contribution to accuracy of the other, less widely used variables. However, the qualitative interviews provide some guidance on this matter.

Although 42% of the polls were weighted by political party identification, the use of this characteristic as a weighting factor was criticized by a number of pollsters in the personal interviews. One criticism is that such weighting is highly questionable in a period when party loyalties are changing and/or weakening. Perry points out that party identification is not a constant but subject to change in association with changing voting preferences. Similarly, Sussman has found party identification too unstable to employ as a weighting variable. Field used to weight by this characteristic, and in fact found it to be the most effective of all the weights he used up to the 1960s; since then, however, his experience has been unsatisfactory, and he no longer weights by party identification. He and Lewis agree that, in California at least, party registration is now a poor indicator of voting preference. It seems likely that the use of party identification as a weighting variable is of limited, if any, value despite its "intuitive" attractiveness.

Closely related to party identification as a possible weighting variable is past voting behavior, that is, how often respondents report they have voted in the past and for whom. During the 1960s and into the 1970s, a number of pollsters employed this characteristic regularly. Currently, it has fallen into disuse. The reported problem with it is twofold. First is the inflated proportion of respondents who claim to have voted in past elections, and second is a postelection bandwagon effect, with the winner in the previous election receiving a larger claimed vote in surveys than is actually the case. Perry reports that unpublished analyses con-

ducted as early as the 1940s for the Gallup Poll by the late Ed Benson showed that a considerable part of the excess claimed votes for a winning candidate came from nonvoters claiming to have voted and saying they voted for the winner. However, other pollsters apparently did not identify this phenomenon until much later. Traugott confirms that more recent survey data from Michigan voting behavior studies show a similar pattern.

A commonly related experience is that the reported education of respondents in polls is higher than would be expected on the basis of census data. Since education is an important correlate of voting behavior, some pollsters believe that this discrepancy makes it imperative to use education as a weighting variable. (Education was used as a weighting variable in 26% of the polls in the quantitative survey.) Perry is strongly committed to its use and reports that weighting by education is a basic correction that has significantly contributed to the accuracy of national Gallup Polls over the years. His practice was to control for education within a matrix that also included region and sex. Because of the historically large differences in education by sex and region, he thinks using such a weighting matrix is essential.

A problem in using education as a weighting factor is reported by Meyer. He found in North Carolina that after he weighted by education, his sample overrepresented Democrats. He feels that one possible source of difficulty when weighting by education in a state like North Carolina is a strong correlation between age and party identification. If a sample is weighted sequentially, as is common practice, and correlated weighting variables are used, the danger of overcorrecting sample bias becomes real. Perry's practice of using a matrix that controls education by other correlated characteristics is one way of avoiding this danger.

Some pollsters, such as Roper, have speculated that census data on educational attainment may be less valid than such data obtained in sample surveys. They suspect that many respondents may be less than candid when reporting socioeconomic characteristics such as education (and income) to a government interviewer. No data supporting this suspicion were cited, and pollsters like Perry reject it, pointing out that the educational composition of poll samples approaches census data when a full schedule of call-backs is conducted. In any event, this suspicion

helps explain why many pollsters do not use education as a weighting factor despite its correlation with voting behavior.

Standard polling procedure is to interview only one person in a household regardless of the number of voting-age adults residing there. Although it is necessary to weight by size of household to correct for the resultant unequal probability of selection, this is seldom done. As noted above, only 14% of the polls in the quantitative surveys were conducted by organizations that do so. Among the pollsters personally interviewed, Black, Mitofsky, and Perry reported that they use this procedure. Mitofsky is highly critical of the failure of most other pollsters to use this variable, deeming it symptomatic of low standards. Perry reports that unpublished analyses conducted in the 1960s show that in national elections weighting by size of household increased the share of preference for Democratic candidates by about 0.8 points—adding to poll accuracy in that time period.

Although weighting by regional voting strength is not common, this procedure had been used as early as the mid-1930s. Perry reports that since 1936 the Gallup Poll has employed regional weights in its national pre-election polls and that this has contributed significantly to its accuracy record. This procedure was especially important with respect to the South since its turnout has historically been appreciably lower than that of the rest of the country.

An important value of weighting by regional voting strength is that methods for identifying likely voters reportedly do not necessarily fully correct for regional variations in turnout. Perry found that if he relied only on his method for identifying likely voters, in both presidential and off-year elections since 1950, the South would have been disproportionately represented in pre-election polls. Roberts reports that in an Iowa election in which abortion was an issue, Dubuque County (which has a large Catholic population) had a larger turnout than was indicated by his likely voter definition, adversely affecting poll accuracy. In 1982, Morris and I, following up on questions raised by news reporter E. J. Dionne, found that in the 1982 New York gubernatorial election, relying only on a likely voter screen did not effect much change in the population ratio of city to state, whereas historically the city's share of the total vote was considerably less than its population

weight (unpublished analyses). Reweighting likely voters in the sample in line with historical voting patterns correctly reduced Cuomo's lead over Lehrman by 6 points.

Taylor suggests that one reason likely voter screens do not control for geographic differences in turnout is that they can work differently in areas with different political cultures. For example, the practice of voting may be more firmly established in some areas than in others, so that similar expressions of intent to vote may not translate equally into behavior. Also, institutional barriers and facilitators to registering and voting often differ regionally. Tuchfarber believes that this may be the case in some states, but claims that in Ohio the political culture varies little so far as turnout is concerned, so that the distribution of the voting population closely parallels the distribution of the voting-age population. In such instances, weighting by geographic differences in turnout rates could not be expected to contribute to poll accuracy.

CALL-BACKS

Although making repeated call-backs to maximize completion rates is an essential aspect of probability sampling, call-backs were seldom if ever conducted in pre-election polls until the advent of telephone interviewing. Cost and the use of nonprobability designs are two important reasons why that was the case. Another reason, still pertinent in telephone polls, is the desire to complete pre-election polls within a narrow time frame. It was impractical to schedule call-backs in personal interview surveys since weeks rather than days would be needed to complete a full schedule of call-backs. Telephone interviewing has made call-backs practical in terms of both time and cost. Nonetheless, despite the fact that 86% of the polls in the quantitative survey were conducted by polling organizations that use some kind of random telephone number generation, 31% were conducted by pollsters who, as a matter of standard procedure, do not conduct call-backs (see Table 3.10). Instead, they conduct interviewing on weekday nights or weekends, when the largest proportion of voting-age adults is likely to be at home (see Table 3.11). (Those who conduct call-backs also typically concentrate their interviewing during those times.)

TABLE 3.10 / HANDLING NOT-AT-HOMES

Method Used	All Polls (%)	Accuracy Tercile		
		High (%)	Medium (%)	Low (%)
Conduct call-backs	64	77	72	61
Substitute	11	8	11	14
Use more than one method	7	4	6	11
Weight by times at home	*	—	—	—
None of the above	13	11	11	14
Total	100	101[†]	100	100
Number of polls	(347)	(114)	(120)	(104)

*Less than 1%.
[†]Total is more than 100% because of rounding.

Pollsters who conduct call-backs report that this procedure has resulted in the reduction of what could be a significant political bias. Clymer's experience is that when call-backs are not conducted, Democrats are underrepresented in the obtained sample. Sussman also reports that one-call samples get too few Democrats, adding the observation that there is less variability in unweighted three-call samples than in unweighted one-call samples. Wetzel and Epstein, however, question the practical value of repeated call-backs. They claim that the main effect of call-backs is to increase the percentage of undecided without any noticeable improvement in sample quality. Similarly, Rappeport observes that respondents reached in call-back interviews are disproportionately nonvoters. In opposition to this contention, Black reports that in a postelection analysis of data on the 1984 presidential election, by using data from a full sample based on four calls the margin of victory was correctly 6 points narrower than it would have been had he used data based on one call.

The issue appears to be not so much whether call-backs make a difference in the composition of the obtained sample as whether the difference is worth it. Those pollsters like Wetzel, Epstein, and Rappeport who believe that call-backs are not worth it assert that the sample gain is predominantly among those who eventually are screened out as likely nonvoters, so little is lost by their not being included in the unscreened sample. Turning to the quantita-

TABLE 3.11 / INTERVIEWING HOURS

		Accuracy Tercile		
Interviewing Hours	All Polls (%)	High (%)	Medium (%)	Low (%)
Saturdays	82	77	88	81
Sundays	73	69	78	71
Weekday, evenings only	73	73	72	73
Weekday, daytime and evening	27	27	27	27
Weekday, daytime only	—	—	—	—
Total*	255	246	265	252
Number of polls	(347)	(114)	(120)	(104)

*Totals are more than 100% because of multiple responses.

tive survey, a comparison of the accuracy of polls conducted by those who make call-backs and those who do not shows that the former are more accurate to a degree that borders on significance: 37% are in the high-accuracy tercile, compared with 26% of all those who do not (see Table 3.12).

One reason a more clear-cut distinction does not exist between the accuracy of polls that are based on call-backs and those that are not may be the variability in call-back methodology. This variability reflects different approaches to completing a poll within the shortest possible time period: Meyer obtains 80% of his sample within a four-day period. Mitofsky normally allows about four or five days for interviewing in order to make up to four calls. Lewis

TABLE 3.12 / ACCURACY AND CALL-BACKS

Accuracy Tercile	Conducts Call-Backs (%)	Substi-tutes (%)	Uses More Than One Method (%)	Uses None of the Above (%)
High	37	25	17	32
Medium	37	36	31	32
Low	26	39	52	36
Total	100	100	100	100
Number of polls	(238)	(36)	(23)	(41)

limits his call-back schedule to two calls in order to complete interviewing within a very tight schedule, while Sussman will normally conduct up to three calls. Field normally allows seven to eight nights to complete a poll in order to achieve a 50%–55% completion rate. Ferree will substitute if after four calls an interview has not been completed.

The quantitative survey did not determine how many call-backs were conducted, so the relation of accuracy to number of calls, and to completion rates, cannot be ascertained. Yet, it seems reasonable to infer on the basis of the available data that conducting repeated call-backs to achieve a high completion rate within a narrow time frame will contribute to poll accuracy. Thus, the use of insufficient call-backs is probably one reason why quota samples performed so well relative to nonquota samples. As for call-backs resulting in an increased representation of nonvoters in samples, the efficacy of call-backs is contingent upon having a good method for distinguishing between likely voters and nonvoters; if methods for making this distinction are inadequate (which, as discussed later, is a problem), it is conceivable that a one-call sample might produce a sample of likely voters that approximates what would be produced by a multicall sample. The choice seems to come down to relying upon compensating biases, always risky, or developing an accurate method for identifying likely voters to use in conjunction with a schedule of repeated call-backs.

ACCESSIBILITY AND REFUSAL RATES

Achieving high completion rates is determined by accessibility of the survey population as well as by the number of call-backs that are made. A generally accepted methodological advantage of telephone surveys is the improved access they offer. A number of pollsters observed that telephoning improved access in low-income areas. Since such areas can be extremely difficult to cover in personal interview surveys, this improved access can compensate for the sample bias resulting from the loss of low-income nontelephone households. Telephone interviewing also improves access to households in high-rise apartment buildings, which restrict entry to interviewers. And telephone surveys also facilitate

interviewing in the evening, when most adults are most easily reached. (Of the polls in the quantitative survey, 73% were conducted by organizations that interview on weekday evenings.) A number of pollsters also pointed out that telephone surveys allow for the completion of interviewing during narrow time frames even when the weather is bad.

Counteracting the increased access provided by the telephone is the greater suspicion and resistance often encountered. The widespread use of the telephone for selling is one frequently cited reason for this resistance. Also, the fact that telephone surveys are relatively easy to conduct has led to a proliferation that some pollsters believe is antagonizing many people. Another source of resistance specific to pre-election polling mentioned by Timberlake and Kohut is suspicion that a poll may be sponsored by a partisan group. The fear in this instance is that one's voting preference will become known to a local political organization. Perry concurs that especially within the context of a local election, protecting anonymity can be crucial in pre-election polling. Suspicion about respondent selection procedures, discussed in the next section, is also a source of resistance that reportedly adds appreciably to refusal rates in telephone polls.

In any event, high refusal rates in telephone surveys are reported by numerous pollsters. For example, Garcia has experienced refusal rates of 30%, Merrill of 30%–50%, and Meyer a 25% refusal rate out of an overall noncompletion rate of one-third. Sizable sample biases can be a serious problem with refusal rates of this magnitude, even with what would otherwise be a well-designed and well-executed probability sample. Thus, the comparability in the accuracy of quota and nonquota samples discussed earlier may in part be due to sample biases caused by high refusal rates. Teeter concludes that the improved accessibility provided by the telephone is largely canceled out by the high refusal rates that characterize them.

Black reports that he has been able to control the refusal problem to some extent by conducting "conversion" call-backs. Attempting to convert refusals is more practical by telephone than in person, for reasons of time, cost, and the availability of qualified interviewers (see Table 3.13). Nonetheless, 82% of the polls in the quantitative survey were conducted by organizations that do not

TABLE 3.13 / HANDLING REFUSALS

		Accuracy Tercile		
Attempts to Convert Refusals	All Polls (%)	High (%)	Medium (%)	Low (%)
Conversion attempted as standard procedure	13	17	9	14
Conversion attempted for some elections	5	7	2	9
Conversion not attempted	82	76	89	77
Total	100	100	100	100
Number of polls	(347)	(114)	(120)	(104)

attempt to convert refusals in their pre-election polls. Black's experience in pre-election polls with initial refusal rates of 18%–25% is that about one-fifth to one-fourth can be converted. Kohut also reports reasonable success in conducting conversion interviews in pre-election polls. In fact, he feels that converting refusals may contribute more to poll accuracy than does a random selection of respondents within a household.

In the quantitative survey, polls conducted by organizations that attempt refusal conversions were more accurate than other polls (42% versus 32%), but the difference is not statistically significant (see Table 3.14). One likely reason the difference is not greater is that even those organizations that do attempt conversions do not do so as standard operating procedure. Nonetheless,

TABLE 3.14 / ACCURACY AND CONVERSION ATTEMPTS

	Attempted Conversion			Conversion Never Attempted (%)
Accuracy Tercile	Total (%)	Standard (%)	Sometimes (%)	
High	42	42	42	32
Medium	20	25	11	39
Low	38	33	47	29
Total	100	100	100	100
Number of polls	(64)	(45)	(19)	(274)

TABLE 3.15 / RESPONDENT SELECTION PROCEDURES

| | | Accuracy Tercile | | |
Respondent Selection	All Polls (%)	High (%)	Medium (%)	Low (%)
Available voting-age adult	41	40	43	39
Youngest man/woman at home	28	38	24	22
Random selection from listing of household members	18	17	15	25
Next-birthday procedure	13	5	18	14
Total	100	100	100	100
Number of polls	(347)	(114)	(120)	(104)

it seems likely that a combination of repeated call-backs and attempts to convert refusals would, by improving completion rates, add to poll accuracy. Unfortunately, the rarity of refusal conversion makes it impossible to draw any conclusions as to how much improvement in accuracy would result.

RESPONDENT SELECTION

Deviation from probability sampling in the selection of which member of the household to interview is widespread in pre-election polling (see Table 3.15). Of the polls in the quantitative survey, 41% were conducted by organizations that interview any available adult. Another 28% were conducted by organizations that ask to speak to the youngest man or to the youngest or oldest woman at home, a nonrandom procedure that controls the selection process without imposing any quota other than for sex. A total of 31% were conducted by organizations that use some form of random respondent selection—18% by selecting randomly from a household listing and 13% by using the next-birthday method. Convenience, cost considerations, the desire to avoid negative respondent reactions to interviews that start off with household listings, and the tight time frames in which pre-election polls are conducted account for the limited use of nonprobability respondent selection procedures.

TABLE 3.16 / ACCURACY AND RESPONDENT SELECTION

Accuracy Tercile	Available Voting-Age Adult (%)	Youngest Man/Woman at Home (%)	Random Household Listing (%)	Next-Birthday Procedure (%)
High	33	46	30	14
Medium	38	30	29	51
Low	29	24	41	35
Total	100	100	100	100
Number of polls	(136)	(96)	(63)	(43)

Interviewing available adults is not only a theoretically flawed procedure; pollsters who have used it report that it systematically produces a sample imbalanced by sex, with women consistently overrepresented (see Table 3.16). Nonetheless, polls conducted by organizations that interview any available adult are about as likely to be in the high-accuracy tercile (33%) as are those that randomly select respondents from household listings (30%). It seems likely that the relative accuracy of polls in which any available adult is interviewed may be accounted for, at least in part, by the application of sample weights that adjust for sex and other sample biases. In fact, a number of pollsters who interview any available adult reported that they rely on weighting by sex to correct for an anticipated sex imbalance.

With respect to the fact that polls that randomly select respondents from household listings do not have superior accuracy, Traugott's report that samples obtained on the first call of a multicall sample are subject to serious bias, politically as well as demographically, is pertinent (1985). Accordingly, polls that randomly select respondents but do not make sufficient call-backs to achieve a high completion rate would be subject to sample biases that could lead to large errors in measured preference. That is, the use of random respondent selection can be expected to contribute to accuracy only in combination with a schedule of repeated call-backs. It seems likely that failure to make such a combination accounts for the disappointing accuracy of many polls that use a random selection procedure.

One reason random selection from household listings is not used more widely by pollsters is their desire to minimize refusals, particularly in telephone interviews. Even some adherents of probability sampling are critical of random respondent selection procedures, such as the Kish and Troldahl-Carter procedures, that require the interviewer to list household members individually or to ask for the number of male and female adults in the household in order to select the respondent. Critics of these procedures claim that despite their theoretical superiority, they act to reduce sample quality and also add to costs. For example, Cole maintains that in his experience, beginning a telephone interview with a household listing in order to apply a random selection procedure increases refusal rates. Lewis concurs, saying that the Kish selection procedure is too threatening in telephone interviews, particularly in small and female-only households. Harris Survey experience, as reported by Taylor, is that random selection reduces first-call completions, an important drawback in light of the short time span within which pre-election polls are typically conducted. Taylor adds that the lower completion rates also increase the need to weight obtained samples. Critics such as these conclude that, whatever the theoretical advantages of procedures such as Kish and Troldahl-Carter, they are outweighed by these practical considerations. While none of these critics reported systematic analyses to support their criticisms, the convergence of their comments gives weight to what might otherwise be dismissed as rationalization.

Some pollsters have sought to devise less threatening and less time-consuming ways of randomly selecting respondents without accepting whoever may be available. Hagan has developed a technique that he describes as a constrained stochastic process, in which the age and sex of the respondent to interview is randomly preassigned (Hagan and Collier 1983). This technique eliminates the need to determine the number of adult household members by sex before selecting the person to be interviewed, though this information is obtained later in the interview, after rapport has been established. As yet, Hagan's technique does not appear to have been widely adopted, though it does appear to offer a theoretically sound alternative to the Kish and Troldahl-Carter procedures.

Another recently introduced technique that a number of pollsters have adopted is to ask for the adult household member whose birthday is next (Salmon and Nichols 1983). This technique relies on the assumption that birthdays are randomly distributed across all population segments, so that asking for the next birthday is a random selection. Black, who has used this procedure, reports that not only is it simple to use, but respondents react much more favorably to it than to the Kish or Troldahl-Carter procedure. While it appears to be theoretically well based, the polls conducted by organizations that use it are appreciably less likely to be accurate than are polls conducted by organizations that randomly select from household listings (14% versus 30%). While this reduced accuracy may result from an inherent weakness in the method, the small number of polls in the quantitative survey that use the next-birthday method makes it difficult to draw a firm conclusion. It may be that the poor accuracy record is due to reasons completely independent of the selection procedure. For example, some of the organizations that use this method may not have a good method for identifying likely voters, or they may not conduct sufficient call-backs to achieve a high completion rate. Given the reported operational advantages of the next-birthday technique, further exploration of its utility in pre-election polls appears to be warranted.

A substitute for random respondent selection that has been adopted by many pollsters is the technique of requesting to interview the youngest man or the youngest or oldest woman. It was developed by the Gallup Poll in the 1950s for use in its personal interview surveys. The goal was to eliminate interviewer discretion in the selection of respondents within the context of a one-call sample. A sex quota is imposed, with interviewers instructed to ask first to speak to the youngest adult male at home and, if no man is at home, to the youngest adult female. Typically, the female quota is filled first, and in the remaining contacts the interviewer asks to speak only to a man. This procedure has worked empirically in that a good age distribution is obtained without age quotas, though Perry reports that asking for the oldest woman produces a better age distribution among women than does asking for the youngest woman.

In the quantitative survey, the proportion of polls that are

conducted by organizations using the youngest man/youngest woman selection procedure and are in the highest-accuracy tercile is larger than the proportion of the polls that are conducted by organizations that randomly select from household listings and are in the same accuracy tercile (46% versus 30%). The difference is not significant using a two-tailed test, but the direction of difference is the opposite of what would be predicted on the basis of sampling theory. In any event, the youngest man/youngest woman selection procedure appears to be an empirically useful, though theoretically inferior, alternative to random selection for polls that must be conducted within too short a time period to allow for callbacks. (Since this selection procedure involves the use of a sex quota, a reasonable inference is that the surprisingly high accuracy of quota samples described earlier is accounted for by polls that use it, and that polls that use quota samples with less rigorous selection procedures are low in accuracy.)

SAMPLE STRATIFICATION

The function of stratification in sampling is to increase sample efficiency by controlling variables that contribute to the variance of the total sample. The question therefore arises as to whether the accuracy of pre-election polls can be increased by appropriate stratification.

Of the polls in the quantitative survey, 27% were conducted by organizations that describe their sampling as based on unstratified designs (see Table 3.17). On the basis of the personal interviews, it seems likely that these are primarily local telephone polls in which seed numbers are randomly selected from telephone directories without any stratification; or else they are state polls for which other than arraying telephone exchanges in some kind of geographic order, no stratification was used. Unstratified samples are as likely to produce polls in the high-accuracy tercile (35%) as are stratified samples (37%) (see Table 3.18). The personal interviews cast light on why stratification does not contribute to accuracy.

Few pollsters use political variables to stratify their samples. Instead, they typically rely only on variables such as region and community size that are standard in general population surveys.

TABLE 3.17 / THE USE OF STRATIFIED SAMPLE DESIGNS

		Accuracy Tercile		
Uses Stratification	All Polls (%)	High (%)	Medium (%)	Low (%)
Yes	72	73	73	70
Sometimes	1	2	2	—
No	27	25	25	30
Total	100	100	100	100
Number of polls	(322)	(115)	(105)	(93)

Thus, samples for national polls are stratified by census region and, within region, by some type of community size variable. Practice in state polls differs more. In large states, geographic stratification by county, or by area code for telephone surveys, is common—but with little if any further stratification. For example, Field samples California using census county data and then generates random numbers from the telephone prefixes that serve the selected counties. Some pollsters stratify small states by county, but others do not, especially if a single area code services the entire state. Thus, Ferree formed two strata for sampling Connecticut, whereas Mitofsky sampled the state as a single stratum. Samples for county and local community polls reportedly are seldom if ever stratified.

Since the contribution of stratification is contingent on the use of variables that are correlated with the dependent variable, the question arises as to whether there would be significant gain in poll accuracy if political variables were to be used when stratifying

TABLE 3.18 / ACCURACY AND STRATIFICATION

Accuracy Tercile	Stratified Polls (%)	Unstratified Polls (%)
High	37	35
Medium	34	31
Low	29	34
Total	100	100
Number of polls	(226)	(83)

sample frames. Most of the pollsters personally interviewed assume that having a good general population sample in combination with a screen for likely voters is sufficient to obtain a valid sample of the voting electorate. A few disagree, contending that data on turnout and past voting are very useful stratification variables. (See discussion above regarding weighting by political variables.)

Stratification by political boundaries presents no technical problems for polls conducted by personal interviews. Standard census publications that report population by state, county, and local civil units meet their needs. The situation can be quite different for telephone polls. Stratifying samples by political boundaries for telephone polls, which constitute the bulk of pre-election polls, is simplified when area codes are congruent with political boundaries, such as state and county lines. Similarly, sampling telephone directories for "seed" numbers from which to generate the numbers to call is simplified when directories are organized by county or central city. However, political boundaries and areas served by telephone exchanges are often incongruent. Thus, except through screening listed telephone numbers to determine which lie outside the survey area, a tedious procedure that excludes unlisted numbers, it is extremely difficult to relate a telephone sample to political boundaries. This not only limits the ability to use political variables for stratification purposes, it also makes it very difficult to obtain a proper sample in local elections.

A number of pollsters have attempted to relate area codes and telephone exchanges to the boundaries of large political units such as counties. On the assumption that people know the name of the county in which they live, some pollsters ask respondents for that information, screening out those who live outside the counties drawn into their samples. Lewis, whose sample is drawn from census data, asks respondents for their ZIP codes, which enables him to poststratify his sample by central city, suburb, and rural areas. Mitofsky makes no attempt to reconcile the apparently irreconcilable telephone and political boundaries. Instead, he classifies telephone exchanges by geographic coordinates available from the telephone company, a procedure that enables him to construct a telephone exchange density stratification, which serves as a surrogate for size of community stratification.

Despite disagreement on the part of some pollsters, there does appear to be value in their using some political variables to stratify their samples. One such variable used by some pollsters is size of the voting population as measured by number of registered voters or by turnout. Perry insists that stratifying by turnout is a first principle in pre-election polling. He reports that as early as 1938, in its pre-election poll on the gubernatorial election between Lehman and Dewey, the Gallup Poll stratified New York State to control for the differential in turnout between New York City and the rest of the state. Comparable adjustments were made in other states where sizable turnout differences existed between major metropolitan areas and the rest of the state, for example, in Illinois and Pennsylvania.

More recently, Black reports that he samples regional strata by number of registered voters rather than by total population size. Teichner follows a similar procedure, sampling sections of a state by the number of registered voters. Cole establishes county quotas based on the incidence of registered voters, in effect a form of stratification. Garcia also samples by number of registered voters, but primarily because those data are more current than are census population figures for counties.

Sussman maintains that in states like New York, whose political composition varies considerably by section, controlling for random fluctuations in sectional representation can be very valuable. His experience in pre-primary polls in New York is that such random fluctuations can create the appearance of a shift in voting preferences when no change has occurred. Ferree believes that his use of a sample that stratified Connecticut into Fairfield County and the rest of the state, thus distinguishing between politically different sections, in his 1982 pre-election polls in that state, while the *New York Times* used an unstratified sample, accounts for the difference between the two polls' measurement of voting preference in that year's senatorial race. Mitofsky, who designed the *Times* sample, disagrees, observing that not only is Connecticut a small state served by one area code but that all telephone exchanges in the state were represented in the sample frame in their correct proportions.

Teeter cautions that stratification by past turnout assumes historical continuity. Since that assumption is not always warranted,

he recommends that a measure of whether regional or sectional balances are changing should be obtained before stratifying by historical regional variations in voting behavior. Perry has done that in national Gallup pre-election polls by projecting the secular trend in proportion of the total national vote that comes from the South. While he agrees that such projections are subject to error, he believes that they do provide a way of adjusting for change in historical patterns. As noted in the discussion of weighting, Perry's analysis of Gallup Poll experience since the 1930s is that if the South had not been treated as a separate stratum, Gallup's accuracy would have suffered appreciably.

It seems likely that the fact that most pollsters do not use political variables such as turnout for stratification, but rely instead only on standard demographics such as region and community, may explain why polls that use stratified samples are not more accurate than those that use unstratified samples.

PURPOSIVE SAMPLES AND POLITICAL STRATIFICATION

A belief in the importance of controlling for political variables coupled with the difficulty in doing that in telephone samples is used by some pollsters to justify their use of purposive sample designs. Panagakis is illustrative, saying that polling at the state or local level can be more "expert" than at the national level since one can utilize knowledge of local politics when designing samples. In local elections, for example, he will use past voting data for developing turnout estimates by ward and race and set sample goals accordingly. He then selects a sample of seed numbers from telephone directories from which to generate the numbers that are actually called. Confident in the efficacy of his controls over political variables, satisfied that random generation from a telephone directory sample produces a probability sample, and in order to keep within tight time schedules, he does not conduct call-backs. Thus, he seeks to control carefully political variables known to be highly correlated with voting behavior while allowing the possibility that nonrandom errors will be introduced into his polls. He claims that the tight political controls he imposes contribute to

the accuracy of his polls and that any nonrandom errors in his samples have been trivial.

Claimed accuracy of some newspaper straw polls is sometimes cited as evidence of the contribution that controlling for political variables can make to poll accuracy. Brady, discussing the reputedly good accuracy record of the now discontinued *Chicago Sun Times* straw polls, notes that they were designed on the basis of a very detailed knowledge of what the state was like politically. A sample of individual precincts was carefully selected to construct a composite picture of the state's electorate. Similarly, Link describes how in the final years of the *New York Daily News* straw poll, when, he reports, it achieved a good accuracy record, a probability sample of election districts was used to control for political characteristics. While it was still necessary to use a likely voter screen, he believes that the use of political areal units in the sample design contributed significantly to poll accuracy. However, this sample design had to be abandoned when a switch was made to telephone interviewing. To approximate the controls that were previously possible, he will use highly stratified probability telephone sample designs. For example, for the New York State polls he directed in 1980, he used county and area code boundaries to create eighteen strata, which he then sampled proportional to their voting turnout. His experience is that this refinement adds to the accuracy of pre-election polls and is preferable to telephone samples that are not stratified politically.

Pollsters face a dilemma in choosing between probability designs that cannot benefit from the gains that result when variables significantly correlated with the dependent variable (in this case voting behavior) are controlled and deviations from probability designs that can do so. The paucity of political data usable for designing telephone samples has apparently resulted in most adherents of probability sampling eschewing any effort to use political data in their sample designs. Mitofsky, for example, argues that the use of past voting behavior as a control variable is more efficient at the estimating than at the sampling stage. Such use, however, still requires a procedure for relating units of the obtained sample to geographic areas defined by political boundaries. In any event, the claimed ability of some pollsters to achieve high accuracy with nonprobability samples that closely control for

political variables reinforces the conclusion drawn above that the failure to stratify by political variables helps to explain why polls based on stratified samples are no more accurate than those based on unstratified samples. It seems likely, therefore, that the development of ways of incorporating political controls into telephone samples would contribute significantly to poll accuracy.

CLUSTER SAMPLE DESIGNS

The use of cluster sample designs in polling raises an issue that is in some ways similar to those discussed above in relation to stratification. To maximize the effective use of political adjustments when analyzing poll results, Link prefers creating small, "tight" clusters, such as is standard in personal interview area samples. The political homogeneity of such clusters, in his judgment, would be advantageous in that information about the past voting behavior of each cluster could be used as statistical controls. The impossibility of creating small, tight clusters in telephone surveys is, he believes, a limitation of that method.

The use of cluster sample designs in polling was much more common when polls were conducted by personal interviewing than is the case today. Whereas in personal interview household surveys, cluster designs were unavoidable, unclustered designs are operationally feasible in telephone surveys. Only 12% of the polls in the quantitative survey were conducted by organizations that report they use cluster designs in their polling (see Table 3.19). This may be an understatement because of a misunder-

TABLE 3.19 / THE USE OF CLUSTER SAMPLE DESIGNS

		Accuracy Tercile		
Uses Cluster Design	All Polls (%)	High (%)	Medium (%)	Low (%)
Yes	12	7	13	19
Sometimes	2	4	2	1
No	86	89	85	80
Total	100	100	100	100
Number of polls	(315)	(114)	(100)	(92)

standing of what constitutes a clustered telephone sample. Since there is considerable geographic dispersion when telephone exchanges, or banks of numbers within exchanges, are used as sampling units, such samples might be misinterpreted by some to mean that they have drawn an unclustered sample. In any event, even after allowing for possible ambiguity, the quantitative survey indicates that clustered samples have become less common in pre-election polls as compared with the days when personal interviewing was the norm. Also, except in very large cities, telephone exchanges serve populations that are much more heterogeneous than is typical in area sample clusters. Additionally, cluster sizes tend to be smaller in telephone polls (three to seven is typical) than in personal interview polls (where ten or more is characteristic). As a result, the larger variance of cluster samples compared with equal-sized unclustered samples would appear to be much less of a problem than in most personal interview polls.

Here are descriptions of two computer-generated sample designs used by major national polls, one described as unclustered and the other as clustered:

> The ABC News/*Washington Post* national sample is illustrative of a single-stage, unclustered telephone sample. As described by Hagan, the nation is stratified by metro and nonmetro counties with further stratification by median county income. (Note that although voting data are available by county, they are not used as a stratification variable.) A sample of telephone exchanges is drawn from this array, and one telephone number to call from each exchange is generated by computer.

> The CBS News sample, designed by Mitofsky and Joseph Waksberg, has been adopted as a model by a number of state polls and is typical of clustered telephone samples. After stratifying by region and population density (as measured by density of telephone exchanges), a probability sample of telephone exchanges is selected. A random sample of "telephone number banks" (that is, clusters of one hundred numbers defined by the numeral in the hundreds position of the final four digits) with working residential numbers is drawn. Mitofsky reports that in his polling, approximately 200 banks, or clusters, are used in a typical national poll, with a cluster size of seven. This sample design does not use any political areal units, so stratification by political data is impossible.

Seed number samples drawn from telephone directories may also be unclustered or clustered. In the former instance, one num-

ber is generated from each seed, while in the latter several are generated.

Since there is random error in the selection of clusters, the use of a cluster design can lead to the political distortion of a sample even when a large number of clusters is used. Even if an error-free measurement of the voting preference of all actual voters in each cluster were obtained, there would still remain the random error in the sample of clusters. The Gallup Poll's personal interview pre-election poll, which uses about 300 election precincts as its areal sampling units, illustrates this principle. Checking the actual vote recorded in the previous election for each precinct in the sample, Perry discovered in the early 1950s that the composite vote of those precincts differed from the national vote in some elections by as much as 2 percentage points. Thus, even if there were no measurement error at all in the definition of likely voters and in their voting intentions, the final pre-election poll would still be in error by as much as 2 points. If there were any other measurement error, and that is to be expected, the total poll error would, of course, be that much larger. Perry has used ratio and regression adjustments to control for random error in the past voting of the sample of clusters, but this was possible because election precincts constituted the areal sampling units. He reports that these adjustments have consistently added to the accuracy of Gallup's pre-election polls. On the basis of this experience, the use of areal units for which data on past voting behavior are available, so that appropriate controls can be imposed, is indicated for personal interview polls in which a cluster design is inevitable.

Experience with unclustered telephone samples is reportedly good. When Teeter switched from a clustered to an unclustered design, he reports that he obtained samples that were noticeably improved in their demographic composition, with a concomitant reduction in the need to weight them. He claims that he now relies exclusively on unclustered random samples in local elections, though he does experience difficulty in drawing such samples in multicounty congressional districts. These difficulties, however, seem to result primarily from the incongruity between the boundaries of political units and telephone service areas rather than from the use of an unclustered design.

Polls in the quantitative survey that are conducted by organiza-

TABLE 3.20 / ACCURACY AND CLUSTER SAMPLING

Accuracy Tercile	Clustered Samples (%)	Unclustered Samples (%)
High	21	39
Medium	34	33
Low	45	28
Total	100	100
Number of polls	(38)	(261)

tions that use unclustered designs are significantly more likely to be in the top-accuracy tercile than are those conducted by organizations that use clustered designs (39% versus 21%) (see Table 3.20). However, many of the polls conducted with cluster samples were pre-primary polls. Since, as discussed later, pre-primary polls are significantly less likely to be accurate than pre-election polls, it is not clear that the lower level of accuracy of cluster designs is a result of the design. Still, the weight of experience at this time conforms to the theoretical expectation that since cluster designs increase sampling error, polling accuracy should be greater when unclustered designs are used.

SAMPLE SIZE

Sample size data are available for 355 of the polls included in the quantitative survey. These data indicate considerable variability in poll practice, with most of the polls based on moderate-sized samples, quite a few on rather large samples, and a distressing number on rather small samples. The average size is 756, with a standard deviation of 573. The range in sample size is from 94 and 110 at one extreme to 2,963 and 6,028 at the other. The median sample size is 644; the interquartile range is 405–969; and the mode 1,800.

One factor explaining the high incidence of small samples is that the decision is often made by nonresearchers, namely, news editors. Although they play a central role in determining budgets, many news editors do not understand the need for more than minimum-sized samples. Consequently, as Meyer reports, it is hard to get editors to pay for more than a 600-case or even a 300-

case sample. The editors are aware that samples of 1,500–2,000 are common in national samples and do not understand why smaller samples do not suffice at the state level. Also, many editors want no more than statewide "horserace" results and are uninterested in analytic cross-tabulations, reducing the need for large samples. Pollsters working for local news editors therefore face the choice of not conducting a poll at all or conducting one based on a sample size they might consider minimally acceptable.

Using a small sample is justified by some pollsters who say their avowed objective is to provide a campaign "reading" rather than a reliable indicator of the likely winner. Black's experience is that larger sample sizes tend to be used for polls conducted immediately before an election, since editors are concerned that those polls will be evaluated by the public for their accuracy, than for earlier polls whose deviation from accuracy could be ascribed to changes in voter preference. (For example, the Gallup Poll's practice has been to use substantially larger samples for its final pre-election polls than it normally does.) In fact, there is a small, significant correlation of $-.13$ between sample size and the number of days prior to the election that the poll is conducted (the fewer the number of days, the larger the sample size). Apparently, concern about accuracy does tend to lead to increased sample sizes for polls conducted very close to election day.

Another reason for small sample bases in state and local elections is that those tend to be low-turnout elections. If any effort is made to base the poll on likely voters, a large, costly screening sample must be contacted to complete even 200–300 interviews with likely voters. While this discourages many pollsters from polling on low-turnout elections, it also results in rather small sample bases for many polls that are conducted on state and local elections, thereby increasing the expected sampling error for those polls.

Some pollsters have tried to resolve the conflict between resource limitations and sample size requirements by developing innovative sample designs. In order to get an indication of the likely outcome of the 1982 Republican effort to weaken Democratic control of the House of Representatives without polling in individual congressional races, Sussman created a sample of thirty-seven "close" congressional districts. He polled them as a single stra-

TABLE 3.21 / ACCURACY AND SAMPLE SIZE

	Sample Size		
Accuracy Tercile	400 or Fewer (%)	401–899 (%)	900 or more (%)
High	22	31	42
Medium	41	31	32
Low	37	38	26
Total	100	100	100
Number of polls	(88)	(169)	(163)

tum, on the assumption that the Democrats would have to do well in aggregate in those districts if they were to do well nationally. While this met his journalistic needs, the samples in the individual districts were too small to provide meaningful measures of voter preference within each.

As expected, there is a relation between sample size and accuracy. Polls based on samples of 900 or more are significantly more likely to be in the high-accuracy tercile than are those based on samples of 400 or less (42% versus 22%) (see Table 3.21). But the zero-order correlation between sample size and accuracy — .15—is much smaller than one might anticipate. Furthermore, in a stepwise regression (in which the other independent variables are how far in advance of the election the poll was conducted, turnout rate, whether the election was a primary, the percentage undecided in the poll, whether any contender was an incumbent, the margin of victory, and the polling organization's emphasis on the importance of accuracy, while the dependent variable is poll accuracy), sample size did not enter the regression equation at any step (see Table 9.1). Two other regression models were tested, both of which included sample size but alternately excluded turnout rate or whether the election was a primary. (See Chapter 9 for a full description of these models.) In both models, the beta values for sample size are trivial (— .04) compared with the betas for four other variables, namely, how many days before the election the poll was conducted (.21), turnout (— .13), whether the election is a primary (.12), and the margin of victory (.15).

To interpret the failure of sample size in order to explain vari-

ance in accuracy in the regression models, it should be noted that there is a zero-order correlation of $-.13$ between sample size and the number of days before the election, $.28$ with turnout, $-.27$ with whether the election is a primary, and $-.19$ with the margin of victory. These correlations reflect the tendency to base the decision to use large sample sizes more on editorial judgments of newsworthiness—for example, how important an election is deemed to be as measured by voter interest (large turnout) and whether the election will be close—than on research considerations. Thus, having a large sample may not be an indicator of research sophistication. The fact is that polls with large samples may nonetheless be faulty in other design respects, while smaller and moderate-sized sample polls can be based on efficient, superior overall designs.

It follows that budgetary constraints on sample size can be compensated for in part by such factors as good sample design and good methods for identifying likely voters. Once basic sample size requirements are met, increasing the sample size may make less of a contribution to poll accuracy than other aspects of poll methodology. That is, while there are many polls based on samples that are clearly too small, improving the accuracy of polls that use moderate- to large-sized samples can be achieved more by refining other aspects of research design than by increasing the size of their sample.

SUMMARY

While there are a number of media-sponsored pollsters who utilize probability sample designs, they are in the minority. At the same time, it must be noted that relatively few pollsters now utilize the unadorned quota samples that were prevalent in 1948. Most common are the wide variety of "modified" probability designs, which deviate from probability sampling at the final stages of selection. In particular, quotas and convenience are typically relied on to select respondents within households that have been selected in accordance with the principles of probability sampling. Another related deviation is the failure to conduct a full schedule of call-backs. Despite these continuing deficiencies, the sampling

practices of most pollsters appear to have improved appreciably since 1948.

The proliferation of modified probability designs reflects an acceptance, even if reluctant in some cases, of probability sampling as the standard against which all samples should be measured. Since any deviation from probability introduces the risk of an unmeasurable sample bias, the question arises as to why, despite their acceptance of probability sampling as a standard, most pollsters deviate to some degree from that standard.

Inadequate training in sampling theory undoubtedly is one reason some media-sponsored pollsters deviate from probability sampling. Thus, some pollsters who use probability methods at the earlier, but not at the final, stages of selection nonetheless say they use probability sampling. Limited budgets are another important reason explaining the widespread adoption of modified probability sampling. In telephone surveys, some variations of random digit dialing can be cost efficient, but adherence to probability when selecting respondents, and conducting call-backs, is expensive. Greater media commitment to professionalism in the polls they fund is necessary to overcome these barriers to accuracy.

In addition, there are a number of operational and methodological concerns that account for deviations from probability by pollsters who are well trained in and intellectually committed to probability sampling. These concerns identify largely unresolved problems in the application of the principles of probability sampling to pre-election polling. They include the following.

1. The need to complete interviewing within a very short time frame. This militates against a probability selection of respondents and conducting a full schedule of call-backs. One-call samples, with some use of quotas, have been relied on instead.

2. The resistance and suspicion generated among respondents by the usual methods for selecting respondents in a random manner. This has reinforced other factors, predisposing some pollsters to rely on quotas and convenience when selecting respondents.

3. The difficulty of controlling for political variables, especially in probability telephone samples. This has been used by some pollsters to justify the use of political quotas.

Of the nonprobability methods of respondent selection employed by pollsters, the youngest man/youngest, or oldest, woman procedure seems to be the most acceptable when time restrictions require using a one-call sample, in terms of both its minimal reliance on convenience and judgment and its empirical contribution to accuracy. When there is time to conduct call-backs, the next-birthday procedure and Hagan's "constrained stochastic process" are probability selection procedures that warrant further testing. With respect to controlling political variables, sample weighting is a sound theoretical alternative to stratification.

Although sample weighting contributes to poll accuracy, many pollsters do it for cosmetic reasons rather than as a way of reducing variance. Weighting models should be developed empirically, with variance reduction the decision criterion. With variance reduction the explicit goal, the legitimate concerns of some pollsters that weighting adds to variance would be answered.

4 / Turnout

Obtaining a valid sample of the voting-age population is only the first step in obtaining a sample of the voting population. Each of the next two steps—(1) identifying who is registered to vote and therefore eligible to do so, and (2) identifying who among the registered voters will vote—presents major measurement problems. The importance of solving these problems is indicated by the relation between turnout rate (percentage of total voting-age population that votes) and poll accuracy.

In the quantitative survey, 39% of the polls conducted in elections with turnout rates of 56% or more are in the high-accuracy tercile, compared with 26% of the polls conducted in elections with turnouts of under 33%, a statistically significant difference (see Table 4.1). The zero order correlation between accuracy and turnout rate is − .19 (the higher the turnout rate, the smaller the error), significant at the .01 level. And in a regression analysis with accuracy as the dependent variable and turnout rate one of seven independent variables, the turnout rate has one of the higher beta values, − .13 (see Table 9.2).

Identifying registered and likely voters are problems that,

TABLE 4.1 / ACCURACY AND TURNOUT

	Turnout Rate			
Accuracy Tercile	56%+ (%)	46%–55% (%)	33%–46% (%)	Under 33% (%)
High	39	36	33	26
Medium	36	39	25	34
Low	25	25	42	40
Total	100	100	100	100
Number of polls	(105)	(104)	(104)	(103)

though closely related, are conceptually different. Identifying adults who are registered requires a good descriptive measure of objective status, while identifying likely voters is primarily a problem in developing an attitude measurement that correlates highly with subsequent behavior.

MEASURING REGISTRATION

The accuracy with which registration is measured is extremely important for identifying likely voters, not only because registration establishes eligibility for voting, but also because those who are registered have a high probability of voting. Mitofsky claims that correctly measuring registration almost completely solves the problem of identifying likely voters in presidential elections since in those elections the overwhelming majority of those who are registered vote. Even in elections with lower turnouts—for example, in New Jersey, where, according to Zukin, about 65% of those registered will normally vote, compared with about 55% of the total voting-age population—accurately differentiating between the registered and unregistered voters significantly lessens the problem of identifying likely voters.

Sampling from registration lists is an intuitively attractive solution to the problem of identifying registered voters. (Also, past-voting activity recorded in registration books can be used to classify regular and occasional voters.) However, while sampling from registration lists is a common practice in some countries,

such as the United Kingdom, pollsters repeatedly pointed out that this approach is beset by a variety of problems in the United States. Each state has its own eligibility requirements, deadlines for registering, and, most important, procedures for maintaining and updating registration lists. A reflection of their concerns is that only 3% of the polls in the quantitative survey were based on registration list samples.

Teeter will use registration lists in states that maintain computerized lists that are systematically purged and include telephone numbers and party identification. But those constitute a minority of states. More typical is the complaint of pollsters who have found that registration lists are usually inaccurate and out of date. Merrill claims that as much as one-fifth of Arizona's registration lists is wrong—though he adds that he has found no signs of systematic error. Field would prefer to use California registration lists as a frame for sampling but does not do so since, according to him, the state has a poor purging program, and therefore the lists can be badly out of date. Lewis concurs in this judgment.

There are also practical problems in using registration lists for telephone polls that inhibit their use. For example, Cole stresses the absence of telephone numbers on New York registration lists as creating a serious operational problem. Not only is looking up telephone numbers in directories time-consuming and costly; in addition, registrants with unlisted numbers are lost. The listing of wives' names under their husbands' in telephone directories further complicates finding numbers.

Another practical problem stems from the fact that some states allow registration well into the election campaign (and some allow registration on election day). These practices further limit the suitability of registration lists for use as sample frames in those states. In election campaigns characterized by vigorous registration drives, a sample drawn early in the campaign (which is a practical necessity even for polls conducted in the closing days of a campaign) could be critically biased.

The alternative to sampling registration lists is to sample the voting-age population and screen respondents on the basis of self-reports as to whether they are registered. However, pollsters are unanimous in their opinion that the latter method is subject to bias

because of overreporting, a problem that the Census Bureau has also experienced. Assessing the extent of overreporting is difficult in states with registration lists that are not routinely purged. In some states, according to pollsters, the number of listed names may exceed the number of registrants living at a listed address, since those who have moved or died will still appear. This suggests that overreporting may be even more of a problem than many pollsters realize.

In New Jersey, Zukin typically obtains about an 8-point excess of claimed registrants as compared with state registration statistics. He has also discovered that Democrats are more likely than Republicans to incorrectly claim to be registered, so that he has to take special measures to avoid a Democratic bias when screening for likely voters. Traugott has experienced a 12-point excess in the percentage of respondents claiming to be registered in response to the question, "How about the election this November? Are you registered so that you could vote in Michigan in the November election if you wanted to?" Other question wordings illustrative of how registration is most typically measured are Gallup's "Are you now registered so that you can vote in the election this November?" and the *Chicago Tribune*'s "Are you registered to vote in Illinois right now?"

The claim to be registered is sensitive to variations in question wording related to residence, a characteristic that is not included in the above questions. In North Carolina, Meyer reports that he significantly reduced a 25-point excess in claimed registration by asking whether the respondent's name "is on the registration list where you live *now*." Similarly, in Ohio, Tuchfarber reduced a 6–10-point overreport to 1 or 2 points by adopting the following question wording: "Some people are registered to vote and others not. Are you currently registered to vote at your present address?" In California, Lewis asks, "Do you know for sure if your name is presently recorded in the voter registration book of the precinct or election district where you now live?" Although Lewis's question is similar to Meyer's and Tuchfarber's in that stress is placed on being registered at one's current residence, he reports that inflated claims of being registered are a problem for him. However, a subtle but perhaps significant difference is that the wording of his

question stresses the presence of the respondent's name in the registration book of the precinct in which he or she lives rather than his or her current address.

An approach similar to Lewis's is used by the CBS/*New York Times* Poll: "Are you registered to vote in the precinct or election district where you now live?" Clymer adds that in 1984 the CBS News/*New York Times* poll asked respondents *when* they last registered in states where periodic reregistration is required. Respondents who claimed to be registered were reclassified as not registered if the reported date of registration was earlier than the most recent required date for reregistration. In states that require periodic reregistration, failure to verify when a respondent had last registered can be a source of inflated measurements of registration status.

Also with respect to residence, a number of pollsters mentioned the special problem of measuring registration when polling in areas with large seasonally transient populations. In Florida, for example, it would be necessary to determine not only whether a respondent is registered to vote but also whether he or she is registered to vote from the address at which the interview is being conducted.

A tendency to make a response for the sake of social desirability is cited by a number of pollsters as a major source of measurement bias, rather than such common sources of error in self-reporting as faulty memory. To reduce the effect of social desirability responses, Tuchfarber avoids probing "don't know" responses, classifying them as not registered. He also treats responses such as "plan to" and "haven't had a chance since we moved" as not registered. Lewis uses a similar method in that he classifies "don't know" responses as "not registered." Nonetheless, he gets a consistent overreport in the percentage claiming to be registered. Since there is a problem of overreporting, Tuchfarber's and Lewis's practice of not probing "don't know" responses makes sense. Yet, it appears that not probing by itself is not sufficient to reduce inflation resulting from a social desirability response.

Given the widespread belief that overreporting is in large part a social desirability response bias, it is surprising that only Tuchfarber's question is worded to include a negative response alternative. The inclusion of negative response categories in question

wordings is not uncommon in polling. For example, when asking whether one has voted in a previous election, Gallup asks, "did things come up which kept you from voting, or did you happen to vote?" It seems reasonable to infer that in addition to the reference to residence, Tuchfarber's inclusion of a negative response category is one important reason why he does not have a serious overreporting problem. It follows that the adoption of this technique by others would significantly improve the accuracy with which registration status is measured.

The experience of pollsters in measuring registration status through self-reports indicates that overreporting should be expected whenever broad question wordings with simple dichotomous response categories are used. Specifying the situational conditions applying to the self-report and facilitating socially undesirable responses are necessary in order to limit overreporting. Thus, asking whether one is registered to vote where one lives currently, and verifying where that is, appears to be an effective way of controlling inflated self-reports. It is not clear, however, whether that is better done by asking whether one is registered to vote in one's current precinct or from one's current address. The fact that Tuchfarber, who uses the latter approach, appears to obtain a more accurate measure than Lewis, who uses the former, suggests that asking about one's current address may be preferable.

Clearly, asking a general question as to whether one is registered to vote produces measures subject to considerable error. Specificity in question wording with respect to current address in combination with a negative response category appears to produce the most accurate measurement. In states that require periodic reregistration, asking a follow-up question regarding time of registration is also indicated.

DEFINING LIKELY VOTERS

In elections in which almost all those who are registered vote, not much more may be necessary to identify likely voters than to obtain an accurate measure of who is registered. However, in moderate- and, especially, low-turnout elections, further steps

must be taken to distinguish between likely and unlikely voters among registrants if likely voters are to be correctly identified. Pollsters concur that the most accurate measurement of preference among all voting-age adults can lead to an inaccurate assessment of candidate standing if they cannot accurately predict who will vote. For this reason, they believe that identifying likely voters is as integral a part of pre-election polling methodology as is measuring voting preference. Despite this consensus as to the importance of being able to screen out nonvoters, pollsters also concur that it is one of the most difficult measurement tasks in polling and that it has not been solved by commonly used techniques.

The voting preferences of voters and nonvoters are often dissimilar, so that including nonvoters in the measurement base can lead to considerable error insofar as the preferences of the voting electorate are concerned. For example, Perry found that in the 1964 presidential election, Goldwater's strength was greatest among the most likely voters and progressively decreased as likelihood of voting decreased. Johnson commanded a clear majority even among the most likely voters, so projecting his victory was not difficult; but without a good method for predicting who would vote, it was very difficult to estimate accurately the split in the actual vote.

Some pollsters also noted that the contribution of screening out nonvoters to poll accuracy varies from election to election. They have found that there are some elections in which the candidate preferences of voters and nonvoters are similar. In those elections, it is not critical to identify likely voters. Perry reports that in the 1960 presidential election, voter preference between Kennedy and Nixon was evenly split at almost all levels of likelihood of voting. Thus, in that election it made little difference in poll accuracy whether one was unable to screen out nonvoters. Somewhat differently, in 1980, according to both Kohut and Mitofsky, postelection adjustments of their final estimates of voting preferences among likely voters that were applied to the polls so that they would conform to the actual turnout rate made little difference in measured preference between Reagan and Carter. The two pollsters conclude that the sizable discrepancy between poll results and the actual vote in that year's election was not the result of misidentifying likely voters. This conclusion does not imply that

there were no differences in preferences between voters and non-voters but only that the differences were not so great as to explain the magnitude of error in that year's pre-election polls.

The variability between elections in the similarity, or dissimilarity, between the preferences of voters and nonvoters indicates that poll accuracy may not suffer in a particular election from the absence of a good method of identifying likely voters. However, in a pre-election poll it is not possible to identify whether that will be the case in a particular election without being able to compare the preferences of likely and unlikely voters. That is, being able to predict when a good method for identifying likely voters is not necessary depends upon having a good method.

An important test of the adequacy of any method for differentiating likely and unlikely voters is how well the method discriminates within specific voting segments. Panagakis describes how in the 1987 Chicago mayoralty election, estimates of turnout among blacks ran as high as 95%, compared with estimates of an 80% turnout among whites. He reports that the actual turnout was about 75% in each segment. However, because of the sharp cleavage in voting by race, the overestimate of turnout among blacks resulted in an overestimate of Washington's victory margin in most polls. Thus, having a good method for differentiating likely and unlikely voters can be especially valuable in elections characterized by variable turnout rates for segments of the population that differ markedly from one another in their voting preferences.

Of the polls in the quantitative survey that are based on likely voters, 35% are in the high-accuracy tercile, compared with 29% of those based on all registered voters (and 26% of the twenty-three polls based on all voting-age adults) (see Table 4.2). The direction

TABLE 4.2 / ACCURACY AND REPORTING BASE

Accuracy Tercile	All Adults (%)	Registered Voters (%)	Likely Voters (%)
High	26	29	35
Medium	30	32	33
Low	44	39	32
Total	100	100	100
Number of polls	(23)	(100)	(176)

of the difference conforms to the expectation of those pollsters who believe that it is essential to identify likely voters, but the size of the difference is not statistically significant. The variability between elections as to whether there is any correlation between candidate preference and likelihood of voting undoubtedly explains the lack of statistical significance.

As with registration, the common experience of pollsters is that the methods they use for identifying likely voters result in an overestimate of actual turnout. Furthermore, most of the pollsters interviewed report that the smaller the turnout, the greater the overestimate is likely to be. This commonality of experience occurs despite the considerable variety of methods used. In the personal interviews, there was general agreement that habitual nonvoters—essentially those who are not registered—are successfully screened out. However, those who vote in some elections and not in others are not handled well. As Kohut puts it, "The problem is not at the bottom of the scale—habitual nonvoters tell you they won't vote." The problem is that some variable proportion of people who are classified as likely voters do not vote in some elections. In high-turnout elections, that proportion is small; in low-turnout elections, it is high. Restating the problem of accurately identifying likely voters, it requires a method that first identifies the possible voters and then differentiates between those who do vote in a particular election and those who do not.

There are two components to identifying likely voters: (1) There must be some kind of ordering of respondents by likelihood of voting, and (2) there must be an estimate of what the turnout rate will be. Almost all the pollsters who were interviewed feel they do not have a satisfactory method for dealing with either component. Merrill is typical in saying there is no satisfactory methodology for dealing with low-turnout elections. Indicative of the general state of polling practice, Field describes the identification of likely voters as the weakest link in poll methodology. In his experience, the process of screening out unlikely voters is an "art form," necessary to get the projected turnout rate down to a "realistic" level. Field describes the process as an art form in that he believes that judgment has to be used to decide what is a realistic turnout rate and to select the means for modeling poll results to that rate.

Taylor concurs that "picking likely voter screens is an 'art

form.' " He tests a number of alternative screens, using several internal consistency checks to determine what "makes sense" and basing his judgment on his knowledge of the political scene. He concedes that this reliance on judgment may be dangerous but feels it is even more dangerous to do nothing.

Cole has developed an index of likelihood of voting but says he has little faith in it. He uses it only if it results in a measurement of candidate strength that differs from what he gets if he uses only registered voters who say they will definitely vote. (The latter gives an inflated turnout measure.) That is, when there is evidence that turnout will affect the vote in a particular election, precisely the kind of election in which it is important to have a good method for identifying likely voters, he has no alternative but to use a technique he does not trust.

Alderman assembles several different turnout models—high, medium, and low—and develops a vote estimate for each. Believing there is no means available for correctly predicting the turnout rate, he then relies on judgment to determine how to use the outcome of that analysis. If "all the subelectorates have the same message," that is, if they all yield the same candidate standings, "you are home free." But if turnout affects the standings, he thinks this usually means it will be a close election. He claims that this is what happened in the 1984 New Hampshire Democratic primary.

Two private pollsters, Hart and Teeter, have different methods for identifying likely voters but agree that the precise prediction of voting likelihood is an ideal rather than a practical goal. Teeter uses a battery of questions to rank people by probability of voting. He has validated the method by checking registration books to determine which respondents have voted. Still, he does not think he has a good way of identifying voters. Hart uses what he describes as a "tight screen": registered voters who report they usually vote (e.g., in two out of three elections) and say they are almost certain to vote in the particular election. He reports that 92% of respondents who pass this tight screen do vote, though he does not know what the turnout rate is among those who are classified as unlikely voters. Since his objective is to advise his political clients about voters, he wants to be certain that he has a "good" base of voters to analyze. He is not concerned about possi-

ble error in misclassifying some voters as nonvoters and would rather err in that direction than in misclassifying nonvoters as voters.

Despite their admitted dissatisfaction with current methodology, pressure on media pollsters to devote resources to the development of precise estimates of likely voters is apparently eased by two factors:

1. Current methods work approximately well in high-turnout elections and are seriously inadequate only in low-turnout elections. As Garcia points out, the news media are interested in polling only in high-interest elections, which normally are high-turnout elections. Thus, he usually does not have to cope with low-turnout elections. However, if turnout rates continue to be relatively low even in presidential elections, or if the spread of media polling to local elections continues, the need to develop better methods for measuring turnout may become more pressing than it is now. And the lack of a satisfactory method for identifying likely voters in low-turnout elections can seriously limit academic research in that area.

2. In many, though by no means all, elections, measures of candidate strength do not vary too much by turnout within the ranges pollsters have to cope with. That is, while there may be a difference in preference between respondents classified as "certain to vote" and those classified as "certain not to vote," in many elections there may be little difference between possible voters who do and do not vote. Since the potential contribution to poll error that results from misclassifying possible voters may not be obvious or serious in a given election, some pollsters may be induced to believe that crude methods suffice.

As a result, except in the case of primaries (which, as discussed elsewhere, are subject to a variety of sources of error), most of the media pollsters who were interviewed feel reasonably comfortable with their methods for dealing with turnout—even those who complain that the methods are inadequate.

MEASURES FOR IDENTIFYING LIKELY VOTERS

The methods used for identifying likely voters differ in two dimensions:

1. The specific measures used to identify likely voters: Six broad categories of measures can be defined—eligibility to vote, past

TABLE 4.3 / CHARACTERISTICS USED TO IDENTIFY LIKELY
VOTERS

| | | Accuracy Tercile | | |
Identifying Characteristics	All Polls (%)	High (%)	Medium (%)	Low (%)
Stated intention to vote	94	92	96	93
Reported registration	76	75	81	73
Reported past voting	56	57	53	59
Interest in election	51	56	48	46
Information on election	22	23	19	24
Commitment to candidate	20	15	23	24
Demographic characteristics	12	10	14	11
Other	11	6	10	18
Number of polls	(338)	(114)	(118)	(97)

NOTE: Multiple responses.

voting behavior, future intention to vote, affect (attention or importance given to voting), cognition (knowledge about voting and the election), and values regarding political efficacy or citizenship (see Table 4.3). However, some types of measures are far more widely used than others. In the quantitative survey, 94% of the polls were conducted by organizations that use intention to vote; 76% registration status; 56% past voting behavior; 51% interest in the election; 22% knowledge about the election; 20% commitment to the candidate; 12% demographics; and 11% all other measures. These measures are equally associated with accuracy (see Table 4.4).

2. How those measures are applied to screen out unlikely voters: Three types of application are used—a single item to dichotomize the sample, multiple items used either to develop a turnout scale or as successive screens, and the determination of probability of voting weights for subsets of the sample (see Table 4.5). In the quantitative survey, 47% of the polls were conducted by organizations that use multiple items—29% construct a turnout score; 18% use a successive screen technique; 25% use a single item; and 15% weight by probability of voting.

Of the polls conducted by organizations that use one item, 27% are in the high-accuracy tercile. In comparison, 41% of the polls conducted by organizations that use more than one item are in the high-accuracy tercile. This difference is statistically significant (see

TABLE 4.4 / ACCURACY AND CHARACTERISTICS USED TO IDENTIFY LIKELY VOTERS

Accuracy Tercile	Reported Registrations (%)	Intention to Vote (%)	Candidate Commitment (%)	Interest in Election (%)	Information on Election (%)	Reported Past Voting (%)	Demographics (%)
High	34	34	25	39	36	35	28
Medium	38	37	40	34	32	34	44
Low	28	29	34	27	32	31	28
Total	100	100	99*	100	100	100	100
Number of polls	(251)	(308)	(67)	(166)	(72)	(185)	(39)

NOTE: Categories of characteristics used are not mutually exclusive.
*Total is less than 100% because of rounding.

TABLE 4.5 / HOW LIKELY VOTERS ARE IDENTIFIED

Method for Identifying Likely Voters	All Polls (%)	Accuracy Tercile		
		High (%)	Medium (%)	Low (%)
Develop a turnout score based on a series of questions related to likelihood of voting, and include as likely voters all those who score above a cutting point	29	35	25	28
Ask a series of screening questions, and include as likely voters only those who successfully pass all screens	18	20	18	15
Ask one question about likelihood of voting in addition to one about reported registration, and include as likely voters those who indicate they are certain to vote	25	19	31	26
Assign a probability of voting weight to each person in the sample using characteristics related to likelihood of voting	15	11	15	16
Other	11	12	11	15
Likely voters not identified	1	3	—	1
Total	99*	100	100	101*
Number of polls	(334)	(114)	(118)	(96)

*Total is 100% because of rounding.

Table 4.6). Taking into account the fact that three-fourths of all polls use an intent-to-vote question, it is clear that relying on a single question that asks whether one plans to vote is less effective than supplementing such a question with other items. However, comparing polls that use multiple items to create a likelihood of voting scale and polls that use a number of items to successively screen out unlikely voters shows virtually no difference in the

TABLE 4.6 / ACCURACY AND METHOD FOR IDENTIFYING LIKELY VOTERS

Accuracy Tercile	Turnout Score (%)	Series of Screening Questions (%)	One Question (%)	Probability Weight (%)	Other (%)
High	41	40	27	27	34
Medium	31	36	43	40	32
Low	28	24	30	33	34
Total	100	100	100	100	100
Number of polls	(97)	(58)	(83)	(45)	(41)

proportion in the high-accuracy tercile (41% vs. 40%). These last two groupings are heterogeneous in that (1) each one differs in the specific combination of items used, and (2) a variety of scoring procedures are used to create likelihood of voting scales. It is, therefore, not possible to conclude firmly that the two uses of multiple items contribute equally to poll accuracy. What can be done at this time is to evaluate the measurement problems related to the use of each type of item.

Registration status, discussed earlier, is the key item used to measure eligibility (except in those few states that do not require voters to register in advance). The most common practice is to ask a single question to measure registration status, though, as noted above, some pollsters ask supplemental questions on time of registration and length of residence at current address to increase precision.

Primaries present special problems for determining eligibility to vote since, with the exception of open-primary states, it is necessary to determine in which party's primary the respondent can vote if he or she wants to. To sample Republicans and Democrats separately, Teeter has created his own lists of registered voters by reprocessing computerized state lists. This is costly—financing has been provided by his political clients—and it is not likely that media polls will ever have the resources for such an operation. Instead, they must rely on self-reports regarding party of registration. Teichner, for example, screens all voting-age respondents for registration status and then asks for party of registration.

Black points out that it is not sufficient to ask in what party one is registered in the sixteen states that do not require party registration. This system creates a free-floating electorate whose members can opt to vote in whatever primary they choose. To deal with this problem, pollsters have developed additional questions to allocate independents to one party or the other. Polling in states that permit voters registered in one party to vote in another party's primary is even more complicated.

The importance of independent and crossover voting in primaries is evident in Panagakis's experience in the 1984 Illinois Democratic presidential primary. He found that while Mondale's strength remained constant among registered Democrats, there was a trend away from Hart among other voters. If he had polled only registered Democrats, he would have had a sizable error. Tuchfarber also emphasizes the difficulties that crossover voting creates when polling in primaries. He contrasts the ability of four Ohio polls to correctly indicate a Reagan victory in 1984 by about 18–19 points with their incorrect indication that Mondale would defeat Hart in that spring's Democratic primary. While a failure to pick up a last-minute trend may account for the error in the primary, Tuchfarber thinks that inadequate methods for coping with crossover voting is responsible. In future pre-primary polls, he plans to ask for party identification as well as registration status.

While asking for party identification may add to accuracy, the experience of other pollsters suggests that a more detailed method is needed. Taylor notes that "tactical" voting by loyalists of one party who seek to influence the candidate selection of the opposition party must be taken into account. A question that determines which party's primary one intends to vote in, regardless of party of registration or identification, must also be asked in states that allow crossover voting.

Intention to vote in an election is an almost universally used item to identify likely voters. The general experience is that a simple question asking whether one plans to vote produces a gross overestimate of the size of the likely voter population. Some pollsters are willing to accept this, arguing that in high-turnout elections this overestimate makes little difference, while in low-turnout elections no method works satisfactorily. Others seek refinement by using some type of rating scale to measure likelihood

of voting. Four-point verbal scales are used by some pollsters, for example, Panagakis and Cole, while others, such as Meyer and Ferree, prefer to use scales with more than four points—sometimes as many as ten or eleven points. The latter claim that using rating scales with many points has helped but that when they rely only on the rating scale, they still overestimate turnout—especially in low-turnout elections. Pollsters who rely on a rating scale as their only item other than registration status for identifying likely voters typically classify as likely voters only those respondents who select the top scale position, for example, "absolutely certain will vote." This practice is based on the belief that anyone who voices any uncertainty about voting is unlikely to vote.

Lewis adds a different twist to measuring intent to vote by adding the phrase "or wouldn't you vote" to the question that asks for candidate preference. Doing this takes advantage of the fact, discussed later, that a large share of undecided voters do not vote. By allowing respondents to classify themselves as nonvoters instead of voicing a preference, Lewis does not have to filter out undecided nonvoters at another stage.

The fact that intent to vote overestimates the proportion of voting-age adults that does vote illustrates the elementary principle that behavior is the outcome of more than simple intent. At a minimum, situational constraints upon behavior must be taken into account. With respect to voting, we have already discussed the most obvious situational constraint, whether one has qualified himself or herself to vote by registering. What is needed in addition is a means for discriminating between "absolutely certain" registered voters who will vote in a given election and those who will not. Using additional correlates of likelihood of voting is needed to achieve that.

A major correlate of voting likelihood is past turnout—Mitofsky believes that relying on past behavior is the single most effective way of controlling for turnout among registered voters. Two general approaches for utilizing past voting behavior were described in the personal interviews. One, the more common, is to ask respondents about their frequency of voting. Some pollsters do this by asking a general question as to how often one votes; others ask how many times one has voted out of the last four elections; and still others ask whether one voted in the last election. There is

also variety in terms of whether the question asks about elections in general or about a specific type of election, for example, gubernatorial or primaries. Also, some pollsters ask a number of questions to measure past behavior, while others rely on a single question. While no evidence is available as to the relative efficacy of these variations, the gains in reducing inflated claimed registration that have been achieved by specifying the context of the question suggest that specifying the number of elections one has voted in by type of election will be the most effective method.

The second approach, used by Mitofsky, has not been widely adopted. Taking advantage of the University of Michigan's National Election Studies (NES), in which registration books have been checked to determine which respondents voted, he has calculated turnout rates for demographic cells. He then uses those rates as cell weights to adjust his sample for turnout (Traugott and Tucker 1984). One advantage of this procedure, as described by Mitofsky, is that the entire sample is used. This contrasts with other methods that significantly reduce the effective sample size by screening out likely nonvoters. Particularly in low-turnout elections, this could add to a poll's statistical efficiency. A limitation of this method is that since the data used to develop the weighting model come from the NES, they are available only for national elections. Other methods must be relied on for state and local elections and for primaries

A small number of polls in the quantitative survey were conducted by organizations that assign a probability of voting weight to each respondent using characteristics related to likelihood of voting. It is not possible to determine whether other pollsters who weight by probability of voting used Mitofsky's method. Consequently, a valid comparison of his approach with others is not possible. Overall, polls conducted by organizations that weight by probability of voting were no more likely to be in the high-accuracy tercile than those conducted by organizations that rely on a single item (27% in both cases).

A number of pollsters caution against relying too heavily on past behavior (almost half the polls in the quantitative survey were conducted by organizations that do not use past voting behavior to identify likely voters). They are concerned that provision must be made for changes in turnout rates from historical patterns

and for new voters—both those previously too young to vote and newly registered older voters. For example, Sussman, who is reluctant to assume persistence of past voting patterns, tests different turnout rates for demographic cells to determine how much difference alternative turnout assumptions make in estimating candidate strength. Kohut suspects that past voting behavior weighed too heavily in the turnout method he used in 1984, when he underestimated the turnout among blacks and young people. Field comments that relying on past behavior is unsatisfactory because someone who has voted in four of the past four elections may not necessarily vote in the next one. Ferree observes that Mitofsky's cell weighting procedure is theoretically sound to the extent that the assumptions of historical persistence and cell homogeneity hold up.

While reservations about placing excessive weight on past behavior seem warranted, the fact that there is a high correlation between past voting and current voting cannot be ignored. Using past voting in conjunction with other items, such as intent and interest, should reduce the possibility that changes in historical voting patterns will be missed. More difficult is the problem of how to measure turnout likelihood among new registrants. Even though new registrants usually constitute such a small proportion of the total electorate that the practical significance of the problem is limited, some need for a procedure for developing separate turnout estimates for them seems to be indicated.

Affect, that is, how involved and interested one is in an election, is considered by most pollsters to be an important correlate of whether one votes. Garcia contends that the best single turnout measure is interest, seeing it as a summary of all the influences on turnout. More typical, however, is the view that affect by itself is inadequate to identify likely voters, leading many pollsters not to use such measures. Among those who do use measures of affect as part of a battery of items, there is considerable variation in the specific measures they use. Some ask how much attention is being paid to the election; others ask for a rating of interest in a specific race; others for the strength of commitment to a candidate; and still others for how important it is that the preferred candidate win.

The relatively limited use of affect measures and the variability in the specific measures that are used reflects the lack of consen-

sus as to how this reportedly important correlate of turnout can be measured in a way that contributes appreciably to the accurate screening out of nonvoters. Pollster such as Perry who use affect measures typically use them in conjunction with a number of items to construct a scale that ranks respondents by likelihood of voting. That is, affect measures are used primarily as supplementary data that add to the discriminatory power of other measures. The function of affect measures used in this way is to determine whether the "energy charge" of intentions to vote is sufficient to carry the intention through to actual behavior.

Cognitive theory would lead one to expect that voters are more likely than nonvoters to be knowledgeable about elections, so that measures of knowledge would be effective in screening out nonvoters from all those who say they intend to vote. In line with this expectation, Brady reports he has found that in low-turnout, local elections, the proportion of the electorate that recognizes the names of the candidates is typically smaller than the inflated percentage that says it intends to vote. Nonetheless, while a few of the pollsters who were personally interviewed do ask some knowledge questions, they are not commonly used, and some of the pollsters who do use them claim they are of limited value.

Knowledge questions that are used fall into two categories— those that ask about the election process, and those that ask about the substance of an election. Illustrative of the former are Gallup's question as to whether one knows where to vote and Garcia's question of whether one knows the date an election is to be held. Illustrative of the latter are Garcia's questions that measure awareness of candidates' names and the major campaign issues and Black's question that asks for unaided awareness of candidates' names. Perry reports that knowledge of where to vote is a useful component of his turnout scale (described below), but Garcia is dissatisfied with his question.

A *post hoc* analysis of Zukin's casts some light on the limitations of awareness of candidates' names for screening out nonvoters. Zukin applied two methods of identifying likely voters to the same data base, one that incorporated unaided name awareness and one that did not. Candidate standings based on the former definition of likely voters overestimated the vote for the better known of two candidates for state office. Apparently, one candidate was particularly well known, so that even nonvoters were

aware of him. As a result, those nonvoters were erroneously identified as likely voters. When asked to express a preference, they were prone to select the name with which they were familiar, which led to the overestimate.

As Zukin's analysis demonstrates, the effect of media coverage upon knowledge must be taken into account when assessing the efficacy of questions that measure awareness of candidates' names. Extensive media coverage can result in awareness of candidate names even among nonvoters, while limited coverage can make for low name awareness even among voters. Also, ignorance of a candidate's name is not necessarily an impediment to voting. For example, Traugott discovered in a senatorial election that an appreciable proportion of respondents could not name the candidate for whom they had voted even though they volunteered the name of the party whose candidate they had voted for. On the other hand, ignorance of when and where to vote can be an effective barrier to voting, so that these measures might be better suited for screening out nonvoters.

Measures of political values, such as political efficacy and citizenship, are not widely used. Garcia has used items from the Michigan NES studies, such as trust in government and how much of a difference voting makes, but reports he has had little success with them. Similarly, Merrill reports that a question on general interest in politics, as distinct from interest in a particular election, has not helped him identify likely voters.

Roper is one of the few pollsters who reports he has been able to improve his ability to distinguish between likely and unlikely voters by using political value items. In 1984, in addition to asking for registration status and intent to vote, he asked a battery of ten value items. Six of those items enabled him to more than halve the overestimate of likely voters that resulted when he relied only on registration and intent to vote. Those six items asked whether

1. One's individual vote matters
2. Who is elected president makes any difference
3. Not voting is a way of protesting against the choice of candidates
4. One is not interested in politics and is therefore not voting

5. One does not have enough information about the candidates and therefore cannot make an intelligent choice
6. Personal circumstances make it difficult to vote

It is noteworthy that two of these items relate specifically to the election about which the poll is being conducted and not to general values.

Roper classified as nonvoters those who in response to the above items selected at least one reason for not voting—on the assumption that giving at least one reason for not voting is indicative of an inclination not to vote. This procedure reduced the proportion classified as likely voters (that is, registered voters who will vote) from 71% to 62.4% of the total voting-age population. This compares with the actual turnout of 54%. Roper believes that the validity of this technique is supported by the fact that in addition to improved discrimination, it resulted in a 2-point improvement in poll accuracy. Roper's experience not only demonstrates that polling accuracy can be improved by correctly differentiating likely from unlikely voters; it also illustrates the value of using multiple rather than single items to measure likelihood of voting.

Roper data also indicate that the position of turnout questions in relation to the question that asks for candidate preference can significantly affect measurements of likelihood of voting. Roper reports that when a single scale question on voting likelihood was asked after the candidate preference question, the percentage of likely voters was larger than when the scale question was asked first. Apparently, once one expresses a voting preference, it is difficult to admit that one does not intend to vote. On the other hand, Roper feels that asking the intent-to-vote question first would probably make it awkward to follow by asking admitted nonvoters for their voting preference.

That many pollsters are dissatisfied with the methods they rely on for identifying likely voters highlights the development by Perry, starting in 1950, of a turnout scale that has worked very well in Gallup's subsequent national pre-election polls. In light of its complexity and its empirically tested reliability, a detailed review of its development is warranted.

In 1950, using previous research by Robert Coursen that analyzed how voting preferences differed by likelihood of voting,

Perry applied an *ad hoc* scale based on five items—registration status, plan to vote, past voting behavior, having discussed the election with others, and readiness to make a special effort to get home in time to vote if one were out of town—to differentiate likely from unlikely voters (unpublished internal analysis; personal conversation). He then developed an estimate of voter preferences based on the likely voters. Registration books were later checked for a small subsample to validate the scale. The results of the 1950 experience seemed promising, so for the 1952 presidential election, a battery of the following nine items was asked (including some taken from Mungo Miller's 1952 Waukegan study): "how much thought has been given to the coming election; how long resided at present address; ever voted in precinct or district; whether registered to vote; plan to vote and how certain; knowledge of where polling place is; how often votes; how much interest in politics; voted in previous presidential election and for whom."

These items were scored, using an *ad hoc* procedure, to produce a fourteen-point scale. To devise a more rigorous scoring procedure for the 1956 election, all the items asked in 1952 were tested for "scalability" using Guttman scale criteria. Each item retained in the scale was scored on the basis of that analysis, and a summary score was computed for each respondent. The validity of the revised scale was behaviorally tested for a subsample of all respondents by checking registration books to ascertain which of them had voted. The percentage that had voted increased progressively at each successively higher scale rank, from about 5% in the lowest rank to over 80% in the highest. This scale, supplemented by some additional items, has been used in all national Gallup pre-election polls since then, though one of the items used in 1952 has been dropped and a new item added.

All six dimensions of turnout listed earlier are covered by the nine items now included in Perry's scale, making it the most comprehensive of all the turnout scales that have been located. The nine items are:

Eligibility: now registered or plans to register

Behavior: reported frequency of voting; voted in last election; ever voted in precinct where one lives

Intention: plan to and certainty of voting; likelihood of voting as measured by an eleven-point "ladder" rating scale (adapted from Hadley Cantril's self-anchoring scale)

Affect: how much thought given to the election

Values: general interest in politics

Cognition: knowledge of where to vote

Three items were used but have been dropped for not meeting the criteria of scalability and/or added discriminatory power: whether the respondent had discussed the election with others, readiness to return home in order to vote, and commitment to the preferred candidate.

The scale's utility appears to derive from a combination of characteristics that distinguish it from other multiple-item approaches currently in use. First, the comprehensiveness of the scale—compared with the three-, four-, or five-item scales that are typical—adds to its discriminatory power. (Cost considerations probably weigh heavily in the decision of other pollsters to use a limited number of items. For example, Black, who uses six, nonetheless says he would like to be able to use a single item, for reasons of cost.) Second, items are not included if they do not meet the twin criteria of scalability and demonstrated added discrimination. This contrasts with the more usual practice of using items that are judged to be reasonable indicators of voting likelihood. Third, scoring is based on scale analysis rather than on *ad hoc* judgment.

It should also be mentioned that in contrast with academic studies of voting behavior such as those conducted by the University of Michigan, few pollsters have behaviorally validated their methods by checking registration books. In many cases, this is undoubtedly due to the unavailability of resources for this purpose. Sample design features also explain the lack of behavioral validation. The areal sample units in Gallup pre-election polls are election precincts, a characteristic that facilitates checking registration books to determine whether a respondent has voted. The geographic dispersion of telephone samples and the extreme difficulty of then determining in which registration book respondents appear are serious barriers to behavioral validation of most media-sponsored pre-election polls. Also, if only respondents identified as likely voters are interviewed, a practice of many polls, there is

no suitable data base for behavioral validation. Thus, many poll-sters have to rely on judgment in assessing how well alternative methods for identifying likely voters work.

Although Perry's scale has worked well in national elections, he reports that as now constituted it is not well suited for low-turnout elections. The scale does not discriminate sufficiently at the top to be usable in elections with turnout rates of less than about 40%. For better discrimination, additional items that tap attitudes not sufficiently covered in the current scale and/or refinements of cur-rent items are needed.

Once respondents have been ranked by likelihood of voting, the task remains of fitting that ranking to a projected turnout rate. Most pollsters make a subjective assessment of the political scene for this purpose, relying on trends in registration and news re-ports on the expectations of political observers. Trends in voter interest are also used to make approximate estimates of likely turnout. The most ambitious attempt to estimate the turnout rate from poll data with precision is reported by Perry and myself (unpublished internal analysis). In the late 1950s, we tested a number of methods for creating an index of change in turnout from past elections by cross-tabulating two items from Perry's turnout scale—how much thought has been given to the election, and certainty of intention to vote. Weights for each cell created by this cross-tabulation were developed empirically, by testing how well different weights would have predicted turnout in past elec-tions. The following procedure was used: An index of change was calculated from polls for pairs of past elections, and that index was compared with the actual percentage point change in turnout be-tween those elections. For the 1960 presidential election, the aver-age of indices of change from 1950, 1952, 1956, and 1958 to 1960 produced a very close estimate of that year's turnout. With modifi-cations based on further testing, the Gallup Poll has continued to use that method with what is reported to be a high level of accu-racy. Perry reports that in an analysis performed in 1976, the average index of change explained 87% of the variance in the change in turnout from election to election.

Perry has used the turnout rate projected by the above method to define a cutting point to apply to his scale. Thus, if a 56% turnout is projected, his goal would be to measure the preferences

of the 56% of the sample identified as most likely to vote. It is usually the case that the cutting point does not correspond to the distribution of respondents across the turnout scale, so an estimate has to be formed by calculating preferences of respondents at each scale position and interpolating at the cutting point.

Perry has also experimented with assigning a probability of voting weight for each scale position based on the average turnout rate for each one as determined in the validation studies. Voting preferences were weighted accordingly, in a procedure analogous to Mitofsky's demographic cell weighting. This weighting model produced measures of voting preference almost identical to what was obtained when the cutting point procedure was used. Since the latter is simpler and less costly, Perry decided not to use the weighting model. An interesting experiment would be to test whether any improvement is achieved by combining Perry's weighting model with Mitofsky's, that is, weighting jointly by demographic cells and by Perry's scale.

Instead of using multiple items to create a likelihood of voting scale, Alderman uses them as successive screens. Respondents are first asked whether they are registered to vote in the forthcoming election and whether they plan to vote. Only those who are registered and claim they will vote are interviewed further, since everyone else is classified as a likely nonvoter. Additional turnout items—such as certainty of voting and candidate commitment—are asked in order to apply tight screens for testing how different assumptions of turnout rate are likely to affect the election outcome.

This method, in effect, applies a series of 1,0 weights to the sample, with a 0 weight wiping out any previous 1 weights. The screening out of unregistered respondents and those who at the interviewing stage say they do not plan to vote has obvious cost benefits. Yet it can have little effect on poll accuracy, since those respondents would be excluded from the sample base in any effort to limit measured preference to likely voters. However, the all-or-none scoring of additional turnout items makes for a blunter measurement than does the more complicated scoring applied by Perry. Also, while successive screens may contribute to poll accuracy, their value for other analyses is limited as compared with Perry's scale.

POLLING IN LOW- AND HIGH-TURNOUT ELECTIONS

In the quantitative survey, 39% of the polls conducted in elections with turnouts of 56% or more were in the high-accuracy tercile (see Table 4.1). This percentage is marginally higher than that for polls in elections with turnouts between 33% and 55%. However, only 26% of the polls with turnouts under 33% are in the high-accuracy tercile, a statistically significant difference.

Traugott notes that, in principle, polling methodology should work equally well in low- and high-turnout elections since the need for more discrimination in defining likely voters does not change the standards that define good and bad research. Nonetheless, there is consensus among pollsters that low-turnout elections are particularly difficult to poll accurately even if likely voters are correctly identified. There are a number of reasons for this, each related to the need for large samples when polling in low-turnout elections.

One reason given by a number of pollsters for the greater difficulty in polling in low- as compared with high-turnout elections is that in order to obtain equal-sized samples of likely voters, a much larger initial sample must be contacted when polling in low-turnout elections than when polling in high-turnout elections. Thus, for the same level of accuracy, a greater effort is needed in low-turnout elections. Any unwillingness of media poll sponsors to commit the resources necessary to contact a larger initial sample can result in low-turnout election polls that are based on rather small samples. To maintain credibility, poll results are sometimes reported on the larger base of registered rather than likely voters, increasing the possibility of poll error.

Also, as Panagakis noted, when only a small proportion of the potential electorate votes, numerically small shifts among voters can result in large percentage point swings. Given the small effective samples used in many low-turnout election polls, expectations of how much allowance needs to be made for sample error based on experience in high-turnout elections are not applicable to low-turnout elections.

Another source of error in low-turnout elections is the magnified importance of single-issue constituencies. Roberts reports that in recent Iowa primaries the antiabortion constituency ex-

erted an influence out of proportion to their incidence in the total population. In contrast, he notes, the effect of single-issue constituencies is muted in high-turnout elections. To measure the effect of single-issue constituencies in low-turnout elections, one needs (1) a method that validly measures the contribution of issues such as abortion to likelihood of voting, and (2) a sufficiently large initial sample to ensure proper representation of likely single-issue constituents in the likely voter base.

SUMMARY

Although identifying likely voters remains a major measurement problem in pre-election polling, a composite of contributions from a few pollsters indicates that the problem is not so intractable as is commonly assumed. As described above, question wordings that appear to eliminate most of the typical inflation of claimed registration have been developed. Similarly, tested techniques for differentiating between likely and unlikely voters work in moderate- and high-turnout elections. Extending to low-turnout elections the methods used to develop those techniques should be equally productive. What is necessary is an application of resources to that problem. Resources must also be made available to provide adequate sample bases once unlikely voters have been screened out.

5 / Determining Candidate Preference

Polls vary in the specific wording of the question they ask to measure candidate preference, though they share many features in common. Illustrative of the question wordings commonly used are the following:

> Gallup Poll ("Secret Ballot"): "Suppose you were voting TODAY for President and Vice President. Here is a Gallup Poll Secret Ballot listing the candidates for these offices. [Full names for each ticket's candidates listed under party heading.] Will you please MARK that secret ballot for the candidates you favor today—and then drop the folded ballot into the box. (If don't know or refuse): Well, would you please mark the ballot for the candidates toward whom you lean as of today?"

> Gallup Poll ("Open Question"): "If the presidential election were being held today, which would you vote for—the Republican candidates, Reagan and Bush, or the Democratic candidates, Mondale and Ferraro? (If undecided): As of today, do you lean more to Reagan and Bush or to Mondale and Ferraro?"

> Harris Survey: "Now, if the 1982 election for Congress were being held today, and you had to make up your mind, in your district,

would you vote for the Republican or Democratic candidate for Congress?"

Newark Star Ledger/Eagleton Poll: "Suppose the election for Governor was held today and you had to choose right now. Would you vote for Tom Kean, the Republican; or Peter Shapiro, the Democrat?"

New York Times: "If the election for Governor were being held today, which candidate would you vote for—Mario Cuomo, the Democrat, or Lewis Lehrman, the Republican? (If don't know/no answer): Which way do you lean as of today—toward Mario Cuomo, the Democrat, or toward Lewis Lehrman, the Republican?"

CBS News/*New York Times:* "If the 1984 Presidential election were being held today, would you vote for Ronald Reagan for President and George Bush for Vice President, the Republican candidates, or for Walter Mondale for President and Geraldine Ferraro for Vice President, the Democratic candidates? (If don't know/no answer): Well, as of today, do you lean more towards Reagan and Bush or more towards Mondale and Ferraro?"

ABC News/*Washington Post:* "The candidates in November's presidential election are Reagan and Bush, the Republicans, and Mondale and Ferraro, the Democrats. Suppose the election were being held today; for whom would you vote, Reagan and Bush or Mondale and Ferraro? (If don't know): As of today, do you lean a little more towards Reagan and Bush, or a little more towards Mondale and Ferraro?"

NBC News: "If the election were being held today and you had to decide right now, in your Congressional District, would you vote for the Republican or the Democratic candidate for Congress?"

Los Angeles Times: "If the November general election were being held today and these were the candidates for President and Vice President, which ticket, if either, would you vote for: former Vice President Walter Mondale and Congresswoman Geraldine Ferraro, the Democrats, or President Ronald Reagan and Vice President Bush, the Republicans?"

Roper Poll: "As you know, the choice for President and Vice President this year is either Walter Mondale and Geraldine Ferraro on the Democratic ticket, or Ronald Reagan and George Bush on the Republican ticket. As you feel right now, will you *definitely* vote for the Mondale ticket, or *probably* vote for the Mondale ticket, or *probably* vote for the Reagan ticket, or *definitely* vote for the Reagan ticket? (If no preference/don't know): Well, if you had to vote for

one, which way do you think you would lean as you feel right now—towards the Mondale ticket or the Reagan ticket?"

California Poll: "As you know, several people are running for Governor of California in the November General Election. Suppose the election for Governor were being held today. Who do you think you would vote for today. (If no answer/don't know/or unlisted name): The candidates for Governor are Tom Bradley, Democrat; George Deukmejian, Republican; Dan Dougherty, Libertarian; James Griffin, American Independent; and Elizabeth Martinez, Peace and Freedom. If you were voting today, who would you vote for? (If don't know): Just suppose you had to make up your mind today in the Governor's race. Who would you vote for—Bradley, Deukmejian or one of the other candidates?"

CURRENT PREFERENCE VERSUS VOTING INTENTION

One characteristic the preceding questions have in common is that they ask for preferences as of the time of the interview rather than for a statement of voting intention on election day. That is, current polling practice is to ask about an existing state of mind rather than for a prediction of one's future behavior. This contrasts sharply with the wordings used by Gallup and Roper in 1936: Gallup—"Which candidate do you prefer for president?" Roper—"For whom do you expect to vote next month?" For its final pre-election poll in 1940, the Gallup Poll used a wording more like what is currently asked in that it clearly specifies current preference rather than intention for the future—"If the presidential election were held today, would you vote for Franklin Roosevelt or Wendell Willkie?"

According to Perry, an important reason the Gallup Poll adopted in 1940 a wording that asks for current preference is that experience had indicated that many respondents who have a preference say they are undecided because they are reluctant to preclude the possibility that they may change their minds in response to new information or events. Then, after 1948, when pollsters became sensitive to the sizable shifts in voter preference that can occur during the course of a campaign, they came to define their results as measures of candidate standing at a particular time rather than predictions of how people were going to vote. In conformity with this definition of the meaning of pre-election poll

results, they came to rely exclusively on wordings that asked about current preference rather than future intention.

Although all the questions cited above ask about current preference, some pollsters put this within the context of "if the election were being held today," while others use the phrase "if you had to make up your mind about the election today." None of the pollsters had any evidence regarding whether it makes any difference to ask respondents to act as if they were about to vote as opposed to asking them to make a decision about an act that will take place in the future. Ferree prefers the latter approach, observing that positing "if the election were being held today" has a psychic cast that is different from what exists on election day. In opposition are those who hold that although being interviewed in a poll is different from being in the voting booth, the methodological goal should be to simulate the voting situation as closely as feasible. Kohut typifies this orientation when he asserts that if question wordings do not approximate the voting situation, one gets a "soft measurement."

Simulating the Act of Voting

The use of a "secret" paper ballot in a personal interview comes closest to the goal of simulating the voting booth. As employed by the Gallup Poll, using a technique borrowed in the early 1950s from Sidney Goldish, then director of the Minnesota Poll, respondents are given a paper ballot on which appear the names and party designation of the opposing tickets. They are asked to mark their preference on that ballot and place it in a sealed box. The ballots are coded so that they can later be keyed to their respective questionnaires. In the 1960s, Perry extended the simulation by using a paper ballot that, in addition to listing each party's presidential ticket, also included opposing candidates in any gubernatorial or senatorial election to be held in the respondent's state. (This required preparing a separate ballot for each state.) By including the key information for all major races within a single visual stimulus, this technique made for a fuller simulation that, it was hoped, would encapsulate the interactions among preferences for different offices. Interestingly, Perry reports that despite the small sample sizes in the individual states, this technique pro-

duced close estimates of the vote for senatorial and gubernatorial races as well as for the presidential election.

All of the questions cited above name the opposing candidates and their party identifications and ask respondents to select their preferred candidate in a forced choice format that in general parallels the voting act. However, there are some deviations. The Roper question deviates by asking for strength of commitment along with preference, whereas most pollsters measure strength of commitment in a separate follow-up question. Another possibly significant variation is the *Los Angeles Times* wording in which candidates are identified by current or past offices they have held. Also, some wordings give each candidate's full name, while others give the last name only. No data are available regarding how these variations correlate with accuracy. However, giving candidates' full names and party affiliation but not their current or former offices would most closely simulate the voting situation.

Most of the question wordings cited above can be asked in both telephone and personal interviews without modification. However, telephone interviewing makes impossible the use of a paper ballot to simulate the secrecy of voting in a closed booth. Such protection of the privacy of one's voting preference can be especially important in local elections, smaller communities, and areas with strong local political organizations. Timberlake, for example, says that in Chicago's black neighborhoods, reluctance to admit one is not going to vote for a machine-endorsed candidate has been a problem in his polling operations.

The contribution to accuracy that results from simulating the privacy of the voting booth in pre-election polls is evident in Perry's report that using a secret ballot typically reduces the percentage undecided among likely voters to about 3%–5%. He also reports that in 1964, Goldwater's strength was slightly greater when a secret ballot was used than when respondents gave their preference orally. The secret ballot measurement was the more accurate.

According to Kohut, not being able to use a secret ballot in telephone polls is not a problem because telephone interviewing approximates the anonymity of the voting booth better than does personal interviewing without a secret ballot. If his judgment is correct, this would be an advantage of telephone polls. While he does not report hard data to test this view, a study conducted by

Dannemiller of the *Honolulu Advertiser* indicates that using a secret ballot in personal interviews is superior to telephone polling. Dannemiller used a split-sample technique, with part of the interviews conducted by telephone and part in person using a secret ballot. He reports that the two methods produced "radically different results," with the ballot-box personal interviews resulting in "many fewer undecided votes."

A specific aspect of the voting booth that Kohut and Panagakis named as requiring simulation in some jurisdictions is the opportunity they offer to vote a straight ticket by pulling a single lever or making a single punch. Both pollsters report that failure to simulate this feature was a major source of polling error in the 1982 Illinois gubernatorial election. Kohut included the option of voting for a straight party line in the poll he directed in Illinois in 1984, which he believes contributed to its accuracy. However, he neglected to do so that year in Michigan, which also provides for straight-ticket voting, with a concomitant reduction in accuracy. On the basis of a postelection study, Traugott, who also polled in Michigan in 1984, believes that his underestimate of the vote for the Republican challenger for the Senate was in part due to straight-ticket voting on the Republican line in conjunction with Reagan's coattails.

Panagakis supplements the standard forced choice, or "trial heat," format with a "constant sum" question. This asks respondents to allocate ten votes among all the candidates for an office, for example, "Suppose you had 10 votes to cast in this election. How many would you give to Danforth and how many would you give to Woods?" He codes responses to yield five classes: (1) all votes to candidate A, (2) most votes to candidate A, (3) tied, (4) most votes to candidate B, (5) all votes to candidate B. Respondents in Categories 1 and 2 are classified as voting for candidate A, those in Categories 4 and 5 as voting for candidate B, and ties are considered undecided. A comparable coding is used in multiple-candidate races. In those cases, Panagakis examines the distribution of votes to analyze the standing of the candidates between which the respondents are choosing.

The constant sum technique, which Panagakis adapted from his experience in marketing research, is intended to allow respondents to express any mixed feelings they have about the candi-

dates and the strength of their preference for one candidate over the other. Panagakis claims that the constant sum question provides a truer measure of attitude than does the forced choice question. The latter, he contends, results in the inclusion of a floating, "superficial" vote in each candidate's measured strength. He also claims that this technique is particularly valuable in local elections in which the name-recognition value of opposing candidates often differs markedly.

The contrast between the forced choice and constant sum question wordings highlights the difference between two methodological strategies for relating expressed attitude to subsequent behavior. The forced choice strategy, which is the norm in polling, is to test preference in a manner that simulates actual behavior. The implicit assumption of this strategy is that the behavioral context mediates attitudes and must, therefore, be approximated as closely as feasible when measuring attitudes. This strategy also rests on the use of a direct, summary measure of preference as sufficient to classify voting preference. In comparison, the constant sum question is illustrative of strategies that rely on measuring the internal dynamics of attitudes. The implicit assumption of this strategy is that for accurate prediction it is crucial to measure attitudes in their complexity, something that summary, forced choice measures of attitude cannot accomplish.

The rare use of constant sum measures of candidate preference precludes any test of the comparative accuracy of polls based on them versus those that use forced choice questions. However, regardless of any analytic limitations of forced choice measures of voting preference, accuracy has been achieved in many elections using that strategy. Using a combination of summary, forced choice questions as an indicator of probable future behavior and the constant sum method to identify a possible weakness in forced choice preference may be a productive strategy.

Open Versus List Questions

Standard polling practice is to inform respondents who the candidates are and then ask for preference. An alternative is to ask an open, unaided question, so that the respondent's answer is contingent upon his or her knowledge of who the candidates are.

Deciding on which approach to use involves issues of practicality and the validity of asking an open question when measuring candidate preference.

The California Poll's preference question differs from the others cited above in that it starts with an open-ended question. Ferree has also used this technique. Respondents who voice a preference in answer to this question may be indicating a strength of commitment lacking among those who express a preference only in response to the closed question. To the extent that this is the case, asking the open question has analytic value. On the other hand, some pollsters have reservations about the open-ended question, believing that it may give too much weight to name recognition in measuring candidate strength. As discussed later, a number of pollsters have found that candidates who have well-known names, for whatever reason, often demonstrate greater strength in pre-election polls than they achieve in the election. The analytic value of the open-ended question may be negated, therefore, in elections in which differences in name recognition distort candidate voting strength as measured in a poll. A post-election analysis of Zukin's (see p. 152) indicates that such distortion can be a significant source of polling error.

Elections with many candidates, as is often the case in primaries and local elections, create serious practical problems for pollsters. In personal interview polls, cards listing all the candidates are typically used, so as to reduce the burden on respondent memory that is imposed by reading off a long list of names. This technique is, of course, not available for telephone polls, making telephone interviews particularly difficult when polling on races with many candidates. In one local election with thirty-three candidates, Garcia asked an open question without naming the candidates. However, he is concerned about the likelihood that the responses to such an open question will be distorted by differences in name awareness. In another poll, when he compared the results of an open and a list question, he found that the lesser-known candidates did better in response to the latter question. He concludes that list questions are more valid, that respondents need to be exposed to all the candidate names—preferably to see them, as is possible only in a personal interview.

Despite Garcia's concerns, in the quantitative survey there was

TABLE 5.1 / ACCURACY AND THE NUMBER OF CANDIDATES IN AN ELECTION

Accuracy Tercile	Two or Three Candidates (%)	Four Candidates (%)	Five or More Candidates (%)
High	34	30	38
Medium	30	35	37
Low	36	35	25
Total	100	100	100
Number of polls	(164)	(164)	(92)

no systematic association between accuracy and the number of candidates in an election (see Table 5.1). Of the polls on elections with two or three candidates, 34% are in the high-accuracy tercile, compared with 30% of the elections with four candidates and 38% of the elections with five candidates or more. These differences are statistically insignificant.

Question Position

A concern voiced in many of the personal interviews is that asking questions about issues and the candidates before asking for candidate preference can shape the "perceptual environment" and bias poll results. With a few exceptions, pollsters position the voting preference question early in the interview, before any substantive questions on issues or on attitudes toward the candidates. Only 14% of the polls in the quantitative survey were conducted by organizations that ask the candidate preference question after they ask questions on issues and on attitudes toward the candidates (see Table 5.2).

Of the pollsters personally interviewed, the notable exception to asking for candidate preference early in the interview is the ABC News/*Washington Post* Poll. Alderman of ABC believes that it is important to ease respondents into the interview and that positioning the preference question early generates respondent resistance. Zukin and Taylor report that they have found that the percentage of undecided respondents is larger when candidate preference is asked early rather than late in the interview, which

TABLE 5.2 / POSITION OF CANDIDATE PREFERENCE QUESTION

| | | Accuracy Tercile | | |
Question Position	All Polls (%)	High (%)	Medium (%)	Low (%)
Before attitude/issue questions	71	66	74	73
After attitude/issue questions	14	19	10	13
Do not ask attitude/issue questions	10	11	11	8
Ask preference twice	2	2	3	1
Ask only issue questions	3	2	3	5
Total	100	100	101*	100
Number of polls	(339)	(113)	(118)	(99)

NOTE: Multiple responses.
*Total is more than 100% because of rounding.

provides support for Alderman's view. On the other hand, it might be that voicing opinions on issues creates a preference where one did not previously exist. Or it might be that having voiced opinions on issues, respondents may then feel constrained to voice a preference between candidates as well.

Alderman argues that when questions about the key issues in a campaign are asked first, the interview "encapsulates" the campaign. Then, when the preference question is asked, responses will reflect reaction to the campaign debate. Most of the pollsters who were personally interviewed disagreed with Alderman, siding with Mitofsky's argument that placing the preference question late in the interview requires making assumptions as to the decisive issues in a campaign. Mitofsky also notes that for analytic reasons, in polls conducted privately for candidates, preference is often asked twice, both at the beginning and at the end of the interview. Hart, a private pollster for Democrats, follows that procedure to determine whether focusing attention on selected issues changes candidates' standing: in some races it does, but in others it does not. If asking questions on selected issues can result in changed standing, there is a danger of bias when issue questions are asked before the preference question. Hart says this is why he relies on the responses to the early preference question as his basic measure of candidate strength.

The possible bias of asking issue questions before the preference question may have less significance with respect to the accuracy of pre-election polls conducted immediately before an election than might first appear to be the case. Taylor has found that in the Harris Survey, which has asked for preference at the beginning and at the end of the interview, the difference between the two measurements narrows the closer the interview dates are to the election. He concludes that the size of a position effect on measured candidate strength is an indicator of the degree of commitment to each candidate. It may be that early in a campaign, if appreciable numbers of voters are not fixed in their preferences, position effects may be large. But by the end of the campaign, when voting intentions are established, there may be little if any position effect. Alderman's observation that in 1984 the difference in candidates' standing in polls conducted by ABC and CBS narrowed as the campaign progressed implicitly supports Taylor's interpretation.

Black takes a similar position with respect to major offices. He maintains that in major elections—such as for president, governor, or senator—candidate preferences are too strongly developed by the final days of a campaign to be meaningfully affected by question position. However, his experience also leads him to believe that in elections that do not receive major attention in the news media, elections in which awareness of the candidates' names can be important, question position can significantly influence measurements of candidate strength.

Thus, position may indeed be irrelevant to the accuracy of many late pre-election polls. This may explain why, of the forty-six "final" polls in the quantitative survey that asked attitude questions before the preference question, 46% were in the high-accuracy tercile (see Table 5.3). In early polls, however, asking issue questions before the preference question could seriously bias the results. On the other hand, asking for preference at the beginning and again at the end of the interview would appear to have considerable analytic value in early polls.

Among those who say they do not ask issue questions before the preference question, there is no consistency as to what they do ask first. Some, like Gallup, CBS/*New York Times*, and NBC, ask a limited number of turnout-related questions, for example, ques-

**TABLE 5.3 / ACCURACY AND POSITION
OF THE CANDIDATE PREFERENCE QUESTION**

Accuracy Tercile	Preference Question First (%)	Preference Question Later (%)
High	32	46
Medium	37	26
Low	31	28
Total	100	100
Number of polls	(234)	(46)

tions on interest in the election, and avoid all references to issues and candidates. Tuchfarber will not ask a seemingly neutral question such as "What is the most important problem facing the state?" because, he believes, answering that question can suggest to respondents reasons for voting against an incumbent.

Zukin, on the other hand, asks questions such as What are important qualities for a candidate to have? and What are the important problems to be solved? and requests monadic ratings of the individual candidates before the preference question. He considers such questions to be neutral since they do not ask for a preference; thus, they can be asked first without fear of bias. Similarly, Traugott precedes the preference question with a series of items that simultaneously measure recognition of each candidate's name and general attitude toward each candidate. In 1984, Traugott experimented with a split-half sample design, reversing the order of those questions and the preference question in each split-half sample. He found that asking the preference question first incorrectly increased Reagan's strength.

The issue is whether any questions that touch on awareness and feelings about candidates and issues, even those that do not require voicing a partisan position, can be asked before the preference question without some risk of bias. Without more systematic testing than has been done to date, no definitive resolution of this issue can be made. Still, given the concern about bias if issue questions are asked first, the more prudent approach seems to be not asking any issue- or candidate-related questions before the preference question. This leaves unresolved the problem of how

many and what kinds of questions need to be asked to establish adequate, and unbiased, rapport with respondents before asking for candidate preference.

THE UNDECIDED RESPONDENT

The concept of accuracy in pre-election polling is contingent upon what is done about respondents who say they are undecided. How accurately a poll measures candidate strength can be defined only by some kind of allocation—implicit if not explicit—of those respondents who do not express a candidate preference. If no explicit allocation is performed, for example, and the spread between candidates (that is, the difference in percentage points between the candidates) without allocating the undecided is compared with the spread in the election, one has implicitly assumed that the undecided have not voted and/or have split proportionate to the decided voters. *Ex post facto* allocations that use election results to infer how the undecided split assume perfect accuracy in the measurement of those who voiced a preference—an unacceptable assumption. Not allocating the undecided when they constitute a larger percentage than the spread between candidates and/ or than the appropriate allowance for sampling error and then concluding that the undecided decided the election begs the question of accuracy.

In the quantitative phase of this study, therefore, it was necessary to allocate the undecided vote for those polls in which the pollster had not done so. We accomplished this by refiguring the percentage of candidate standings excluding from the percentage base the percentage of undecided voters. This procedure in effect assumes that the residual undecided voters either do not vote or split as do the decided voters. If the reported percentage of undecided voters is small (about 5% or less), this assumption is conservative in its effect on reported percentages for each candidate; but with a large percentage of undecided voters, the procedure inevitably results in a sizable increase in the estimated percentage preferring each candidate. Our use of this allocation procedure does not conform to the judgment of all the pollsters whose results were thereby adjusted, but it does conform to the judgment of the largest proportion of those who were personally interviewed.

Complicating the issue is the fact that the percentage undecided as measured in any poll is to an appreciable degree an artifact of the method used to measure preference. As noted above, Perry found that using a secret paper ballot in personal interviews produces a significantly smaller undecided vote than does asking for an oral expression of preference; and Dannemiller found that the secret paper ballot produces a markedly smaller undecided vote than does a telephone question. It is not surprising, therefore, that polling organizations using different methods often report conflicting results regarding the percentage undecided. Such conflicts raise the question of what is the "real" size of the undecided vote. For our analysis, we used the percentage undecided that was reported for each poll before our allocation method was applied.

Pre-election polls that allocated the undecided vote themselves or reported a small undecided vote are significantly more likely to be accurate than those that reported a moderate or large percentage undecided. The polls in the quantitative survey were classified into three groups, based on the size of the reported undecided vote: (1) small—an undecided vote of 9% or less, with a mean of 4.5%, (2) moderate—an undecided vote of 9.2%–17.5%, with a mean of 13%, and (3) large—an undecided vote of 18% or more, with a mean of 26.7% (see Table 5.4). Of the polls in the small undecided group, 45% are in the high-accuracy tercile, compared with 30% of those in the moderate undecided group and 25% of those in the large undecided group. Allowing for the fact that the accuracy scores were calculated after we allocated the reported undecided, it is nonetheless clear that minimizing the undecided vote contributes to accuracy. This contribution conflicts with the

TABLE 5.4 / ACCURACY AND SIZE OF THE UNDECIDED VOTE

Accuracy Tercile	9% or Less Undecided (%)	9.2%–17.5% Undecided (%)	18% or More Undecided (%)
High	45	30	25
Medium	32	36	32
Low	23	34	43
Total	100	100	100
Number of polls	(143)	(134)	(143)

TABLE 5.5 / METHOD FOR REDUCING THE UNDECIDED VOTE

Basis for Reducing the Undecided Vote	All Polls (%)	Accuracy Tercile		
		High (%)	Medium (%)	Low (%)
Follow-up "leaner" question	76	76	78	76
Party identification of undecided	19	28	15	14
Opinions on issues	9	12	9	8
Ratings of candidates	8	8	9	7
Other	12	19	10	9
Total of pollsters who use at least one method	77	81	76	75
Total of pollsters who do not reduce or allocate undecided	23	19	24	25
Total	100	100	100	100
Number of polls	(353)	(118)	(122)	(104)

judgment of some pollsters, such as Clymer and Tuchfarber, that probing to reduce the undecided requires making assumptions that may not be warranted. (Clymer is also concerned that probing may violate journalistic standards of factual reporting.)

Of the polls in the quantitative survey, 23% were conducted by organizations that do not use any procedure to reduce or allocate the undecided vote. The most common procedure—used by 76% of all the polls—is to ask a probing "leaner" question of those who initially say they are undecided. Next most common (used by 19%) is to allocate the undecided according to party identification, often after a leaner question has been asked. Opinion questions rank next in frequency (used by 9%) and then candidate ratings (used by 8%) (see Table 5.5).

There was no consensus among the pollsters who were personally interviewed on what to do about undecided voters when reporting candidate strength. They expressed three general orientations, with variation within each. These orientations differ in their acceptance of probing leaner questions that reduce the size of the undecided vote and in their approach to allocating residual undecided voters after the leaner probe:

1. Accept any expression of undecidedness in the belief that probing to obtain an expression of preference results in the measurement of nonattitudes.
2. Probe to reduce the size of the undecided vote, but do not allocate the residual undecided since that requires making possibly unwarranted assumptions.
3. After probing to minimize the size of the undecided vote, allocate the residual undecided voters on the basis of available data as to their likely split.

Media poll practice in dealing with the undecided is affected by journalistic as well as methodological criteria. As noted above, Clymer feels that allocating undecided voters involves making judgments that exceed the legitimate bounds of reporting the news. A journalist by background, he opposes allocation, preferring to describe the undecided—in effect, letting readers draw their own conclusions as to how the undecided should be allocated. In the same spirit, when a leaner probe is asked, he prefers to report the results separately rather than incorporating them into a single measure of the candidates' standing. Lewis, also a journalist by background, prefers to give respondents an opportunity to "opt out" of making a choice rather than "pushing" for an answer. He does this by adding the phrase "or haven't you heard enough to say?" to the preference question. He believes that probing for an answer "gets a lot of junk."

Other journalists, however, endorse probing for an answer because they think this enhances analysis. Alderman, for example, asks undecided respondents which candidate they lean toward, telling them that there are no right or wrong answers. He finds that comparing the size of the undecided vote before and after the leaner question, and determining how much each candidate gains from the leaner probe, is a way of assessing how volatile an election is and how certain or soft each candidate's strength is. He also analyzes the demographics of the initially undecided, those who decide after probing, and the residual undecided to identify each candidate's "core support" and to get "a feel for what is going on—Does it make sense? Is it a break with history?"

Doubts about the value of probing for preference exist among pollsters with a background in research as well as among those with a background in journalism. Tuchfarber is typical, expressing

a concern about forced choice "leaner" questions very similar to Lewis's. Tuchfarber maintains that the desire to avoid "missing data" is mistaken and that probing results in false data—nonattitudes. Others take a middle position, not probing in early polls when the preferences of many voters may still be fluid, but doing so in the final poll, by which time they believe a leaner question does elicit meaningful responses.

Implicit in the controversy over probing is the weight of concern one has regarding nonattitudes versus hidden refusals. Opponents of probing, such as Tuchfarber, point to the fact that many of the undecided respondents simply do not have a preference—perhaps because they are uninterested in and uninformed about the election, or perhaps because after due consideration they have not been able to make up their minds. Proponents of probing, such as Perry, contend that a significant proportion of the undecided do have a preference but are reluctant to express it—possibly for fear of expressing a "deviant" preference, or because of the tentativeness of the preference, or because of a desire to preserve the privacy of their vote. Not measuring those leanings, Perry maintains, reduces poll accuracy.

In large part, the resolution of this controversy requires differentiating between likely voters and nonvoters. Perry reports, on the basis of analyses dating back to the 1950s, that when he excludes respondents identified as likely nonvoters, the percentage undecided is reduced by about half in national elections. A forced choice leaner probe further reduces the undecided among likely voters by about half. Perry also reports that in his postelection validation studies, about half of the small residual undecided (about 3%–5% among those identified as likely voters) do not vote, a finding that the reported experience of pollsters such as Mitofsky and Link corroborates. (Perry allocates the residual undecided by excluding them from the percentage base, in effect assuming that they will not vote and/or that they will split as do the decided after the leaner.) That is, a method that effectively screens out likely nonvoters also effectively screens out most respondents with nonattitudes. Conversely, even weakly held preferences of initially undecided voters who do vote count in the voting booth, so they cannot be ignored.

Panagakis's experience in state and local elections, using the

constant sum method, provides a different perspective. He has found that among registered voters who say they are likely to vote, about 2% cannot answer the constant sum question. He maintains that among likely voters it is this 2% who demonstrably do not have attitudes toward the candidates and that this is a truer measure of nonattitudes among likely voters than is the percentage of undecided voters as determined by responses to the usual preference question. Panagakis has also found that the constant sum question typically produces a tie vote of about 14%, as compared with an undecided vote of about 8% after asking the usual preference question. He interprets this difference as indicating that the constant sum question provides a more valid measure of the "real" size of the undecided vote. Confirmation that the constant sum method does indeed validly distinguish between nonattitudes and undecided attitudes among likely voters would be useful.

Link strongly recommends not attempting to allocate the residual undecided after asking a leaner probe. He endorses using a leaner probe because "leaving out the leaners is dangerous." He would not use issue questions to allocate the undecided: "Take the voter's head the way it is because that is how he will vote. Your perception of issues will affect the wording of your issue questions." Short of a method that comprehensively measures the weights that each respondent gives to issues, a leaner question that in effect asks respondents to allocate themselves seems to be the least risky.

Link adds that if a method for allocating the undecided significantly changes candidate standings, "Don't believe it. If it doesn't, why bother?" It is also his experience that many of the residual undecided don't vote, so the problem of allocation is less serious than might first be assumed. Link's approach is, in effect, to assume that the residual undecided (after a leaner question that allows much of the undecided to allocate themselves) either do not vote or else split in a ratio comparable to the decided after the leaner.

Perry has experimented with two nonjudgmental methods for allocating the undecided, with no success. One method compared the views of undecided voters on issues with the views of decided voters. First, he calculated the percentage of voters who favored

the Democratic candidate together with the percentage favoring the Republican candidate, who took opposing positions on a series of issue questions. Then, using simultaneous equations, he estimated the mix of each group of decided voters that would produce the split of opinion among the undecided. His intent was to use the average of the resultant ratios as the basis for allocating undecided voters. However, on some issues the undecided were more like the Republican candidate's adherents, and on other issues more like the Democratic adherents, so that the average ratio was an artifact of the particular combination of issue questions that was asked.

Perry's second method was based on analyses of the effect of leaner probes and a secret paper ballot on candidate standing. A split-sample design was used, with half the sample given the paper ballot to fill out and the other half asked an open question with a leaner probe. Comparing the results of the two half-samples, it was possible to estimate how, in answer to the secret ballot, the undecided split in their preferences after the leaner probe. The hope was that among the intially decided, the decided after the leaner but before the secret ballot, and the decided after the secret ballot, the percentage preferring each candidate would fall on a straight line. If it did, the residual undecided could be allocated from a projection of that trend. While this appeared to work in some elections, such as the 1964 presidential, in others it did not.

Panagakis asserts that in local elections, being undecided is not a nonresponse but a negative comment on the incumbent. He argues that one would expect the better-known incumbent to have an advantage over the, usually, less well known challenger. Thus, being undecided is a vote of no confidence in the incumbent. He concludes that about all of the undecided should be allocated to the challenger in local elections, though not necessarily for presidential elections. Panagakis reports that this method has added to the accuracy of his polls. Further testing of it would be useful.

Traugott uses party identification to allocate the undecided who identify with a party. Undecided independents are allocated in accordance with the preferences of the decided, just as for Democrats and Republicans. Zukin also uses party identification to allocate undecided voters who have a party preference. He then allocates the independents by using monadic ratings they give to each

TABLE 5.6 / ACCURACY AND METHOD FOR REDUCING THE UNDECIDED VOTE

Accuracy Tercile	Attempts to Reduce Undecided Votes						Does Not Attempt to Reduce Undecided Vote (%)
	All Attempting to Reduce Undecided Votes (%)	Leaner (%)	Opinions on Issues (%)	Candidate Ratings (%)	Party Identification (%)	Other (%)	
High	36	34	43	36	51	51	28
Medium	35	36	33	39	28	28	38
Low	29	30	24	25	21	21	34
Total	100	100	100	100	100	100	100
Number of polls	(267)	(264)	(33)	(28)	(65)	(43)	(77)

NOTE: Categories are not mutually exclusive.

candidate, assigning them to the candidate they rate most favorably.

In the quantitative survey, of the polls conducted by organizations that use party identification to allocate the undecided, 51% were in the high-accuracy tercile, compared with 28% of the polls conducted by organizations that do not allocate the undecided (see Table 5.6). This difference is statistically significant. Apparently, party identification can be a useful criterion for allocating likely voters who are undecided after a leaner probe. Whether this procedure produces a more accurate measure of candidate standings than does refiguring the percentage of the decided vote by excluding the residual undecided from the percentage base cannot be determined from the available data. A tenable hypothesis is that particularly in nonpresidential elections, in which party loyalty is usually a strong influence on voting behavior, allocating the residual undecided on the basis of party identification will significantly contribute to accuracy.

To summarize, an effective method for minimizing the undecided vote appears to be the following:

1. Screen out likely nonvoters to minimize the nonattitude problem.

2. Use leaner probes to minimize the hidden refusal problem.

3. Either use party identification to allocate the residual undecided, or, taking advantage of the fact that many of the residual undecided do not vote, refigure the percentage of the decided vote by excluding the undecided from the percentage base.

6 / Saliency, Cognition, and Commitment

Influences on accuracy that were discussed in the personal interviews with pollsters include the office at stake, the "type" of election, how well-known the candidates are, whether an incumbent is running for office, whether the election is a primary, whether the election is being held in an on-year or off-year, and at what stage of the campaign voters make up their minds.

OFFICE AT STAKE

Data from the quantitative survey do not demonstrate any consistent relation between type of office at stake and accuracy. Of the polls related to the presidency, 34% are in the high-accuracy tercile, compared with 30% of the polls on gubernatorial elections, 37% of the polls on senatorial elections, 26% of the polls on congressional elections, and 41% of the polls on other state offices. Of the nine polls on mayoralty elections, 56% are in the high-accuracy tercile, as are 27% of the fifteen polls on county offices (see Table 6.1).

TABLE 6.1 / ACCURACY AND OFFICE AT STAKE

Accuracy Tercile	President (%)	Governor (%)	Senator (%)	Congress-person (%)	Other State Office (%)
High	34	30	37	26	41
Medium	41	32	28	37	29
Low	25	39	36	37	29
Total	100	101*	101*	100	99*
Number of polls	(116)	(57)	(90)	(46)	(51)

*Totals do not add up to 100% because of rounding.

The absence of any relation of accuracy to level of office, or to whether the position is executive or legislative is undoubtedly due at least in part to the interactions that occur when a number of offices are at stake. Pre-election polls typically measure preference in selected races only, so that the way in which being part of a ticket possibly affects preference for a particular candidate is hardly ever measured. (Perry's use of a ticket, mentioned in Chapter 5, is a notable exception and did not become part of the Gallup Poll's standard pre-election poll methodology.) Also, as described in this chapter, the divergent effects of such factors as name recognition, direction of affect toward the candidates, saliency of the election, incumbency, at what stage of the campaign voters make up their mind, and level of information about the election are influences on poll accuracy that are correlated with the type of office at stake. Such correlations probably contribute to the absence of any systematic relationship between type of office at stake and accuracy. Other confounding variables that also need to be kept in mind is whether the election is being held in an off-year or an on-year and whether it is a primary or general election.

Related to, but distinct from, the effect of interactions upon voting preferences is the interaction that occurs when preference in more than one race is measured in the same poll. Morris and I (Crespi and Morris 1984) have shown that under some conditions changing the order in which preferences for different offices are measured in a single poll can significantly alter measured preferences. Nonetheless, judging from the absence of comment on this

matter in the qualitative survey, such interaction effects are apparently of limited concern to most pollsters.

ILLUSTRATIVE TYPOLOGIES

The pollsters who were personally interviewed tended to differentiate elections in terms of (1) how salient they are to the electorate, (2) how much information the electorate has about candidates and issues and how that information is structured, and (3) how strongly voters are committed to their preferred candidates. With the focus of their interest on measuring individual voting preferences, they did not apply concepts such as "realigning elections" when discussing how accuracy in pre-election polls is affected by political context.

Traugott differentiated elections in terms of how well known the opposing candidates are to the electorate. He posited three types: those that pit against each other (1) two well-known candidates, (2) a well-known candidate and a poorly known candidate, and (3) two poorly known candidates. His experience is that each type presents different sources of polling error. He cites the 1984 Michigan senatorial election as illustrative of the kind of problems that occur in the second type. In that election, Levin defeated Lousma 54%–46%. However, the lesser-known Lousma, the Republican, never got closer than 36% (with 8% undecided) in any of Traugott's polls. Traugott ascribes this discrepancy to the fact that the incumbent, Levin, was better known to the electorate than the challenger, Lousma. In support of this position, he cites a post-election survey in which the proportion who reported they had voted for Lousma fell short of his actual vote, while a large proportion could not recall the name of the candidate for whom they had voted. Traugott suggests that this indicates that many straight-ticket Republican voters cast their ballots for Lousma even though they did not know who he was. Presumably, in the pre-election polls many of these straight-ticket voters would have said they were undecided as to which candidate they prefer rather than say they would vote for an unknown Republican candidate.

Focusing on affect rather than cognition, Cole categorized elections in terms of whether voters are attracted to or repelled by the

opposing candidates. For example, he describes the 1980 presidential election as a "repel-repel" election. Cole maintains that the clear negative image that both Carter and Reagan had that year added a strong element of instability to voter preferences and candidate poll standings through most of the campaign. He believes that not until the final debate did Reagan achieve "closure," which set the stage for the late surge in Reagan support. Inferentially, pre-election polls in any repel-repel election would be subject to sizable last-minute changes in preference and, therefore, sizable error.

Ferree emphasized the interaction between cognition and affect in classifying elections and the kinds of measurement problems that characterize each type. He contrasts the 1982 Connecticut senatorial and gubernatorial elections in those terms. The senatorial contest involved two candidates—Weicker and Moffat—who were well known and well liked. The gubernatorial race, on the other hand, was between O'Neill, who had the name-recognition value of an incumbent even though he did not enjoy a high level of popularity, and Rome, who was not as well known. Ferree reports that in the polls he conducted the "attract-attract" senatorial contest was far less stable than the gubernatorial race.

The kind of measurement problem described by Traugott differs significantly from that described by Cole and Ferree. The latter pollsters are concerned about instability of measured preference in certain types of elections, so that no matter how well a poll measures preference as of the time it is conducted, it may prove to be a poor indicator of the actual vote. In contrast, Traugott's concern focuses upon the possibility that preferences are not measured validly even when they are stable.

Another way in which elections differ from each other that was mentioned by many of the pollsters who were personally interviewed is in their saliency to the electorate. In low-saliency elections, much of the electorate is uninterested in and uninformed about the candidates and their stands on relevant issues. Meyer observes that in such elections much of the electorate has no preference and that preferences that do exist tend to be weak and subject to change. Link adds that current polling methods were developed in the context of high-saliency (and high-turnout) presidential elections and that no one has solved the problem of how

to conduct accurate polls in low-saliency elections. For this reason, he believes that polling on low-saliency elections is beset by problems of both stability and validity of measurement.

NAME RECOGNITION AND INCUMBENCY

Name recognition is generally agreed to be an important influence upon both voting behavior and the measurement of candidates' standing in pre-election polls. Still, as is evident in Traugott's experience in the 1984 Michigan senatorial election, high name recognition for a candidate can be a source of polling error. Because of other influences such as party loyalty and the coattails of other candidates, relatively unknown candidates may attract votes from people who would not express a preference for them in a poll. A variety of pollsters report that the relationship of name recognition to voting behavior and to expressions of preference in polls can be affected by incumbency, the visibility of the office at stake, and party identification. Consequently, the effect of name recognition upon poll accuracy cannot be accounted for in any simple formula.

Tuchfarber sees a complex relation between name recognition, incumbency, the visibility of the office at stake, and party identification. On the one hand, his experience is that achieving a high level of name recognition can be especially valuable to candidates for low-visibility offices. Since media coverage of elections for low-visibility offices is limited, incumbents benefit from the name recognition they have achieved from whatever publicity they have received during their tenure. As in the Levin-Lousma election, this benefit is typically reflected in pre-election polls. Counteracting this advantage, according to Tuchfarber, is that party identification assumes increased importance in voting decisions for low-visibility office, something that may be missed in pre-election polls. He suspects, therefore, that pre-election polls overestimate the voting strength of relatively well known incumbents in low-visibility offices. He believes that such overestimation is less likely to be a problem in elections for high-visibility offices since in those elections the news media direct the electorate's attention toward the individual candidates.

Panagakis also makes a distinction between elections for high- and low-visibility offices and the different problems each presents for poll accuracy. He maintains that when incumbents run for reelection to high-visibility offices, voting decisions are based largely upon "job approval," that is, the favorableness of attitude toward the incumbent. He further maintains that in races for low-visibility offices, evaluations of the incumbent's performance are not an important influence upon voting decisions. That is, voters have more information to draw upon when deciding whether to reelect an incumbent to a high-visibility office than when deciding to elect one to a low-visibility office. Accepting this position leads to the conclusion that pre-election polls on races for high-visibility office should be more stable, and more accurate, when one of the candidates is an incumbent.

Garcia also stresses the influence of incumbency and name recognition upon expressions of preference in pre-election polls. He agrees with Panagakis that when an incumbent runs for reelection, the election is essentially a vote of confidence in the incumbent. In such elections, the challenger's qualifications are less important to the electorate than is satisfaction with the incumbent. By adding a known factor to what might otherwise be a cognitively unstructured situation, an incumbent's high recognition should add to the accuracy of pre-election polls. In comparison, when the election is for a low-visibility office and none of the candidates is an incumbent, Garcia's experience is that high name recognition can be a source of error in pre-election polls. In such elections, it would follow, the likelihood is that the better-known candidate's strength will be overstated and the lesser known's understated.

A common thread that runs through these observations is that although being well known is an asset to political candidates, it is also a source of polling error, particularly when low-visibility offices are at stake. On the other hand, the influence of name recognition upon poll accuracy is complicated by the guess that incumbency, which contributes to name recognition, may make for stability in voting preference. The quantitative survey casts some light on this issue (see Table 6.2). Of the polls on races with incumbents, 29% were in the high-accuracy tercile, compared with 38% of the polls on elections without an incumbent candi-

TABLE 6.2 / ACCURACY AND INCUMBENCY

Accuracy Tercile	Incumbent Running for Reelection (%)	No Candidate Is an Incumbent (%)
High	29	38
Medium	36	27
Low	35	35
Total	100	100
Number of polls	(196)	(60)

date. While this difference is not statistically significant, if a one-tailed test were applied to the hypothesis that polls on elections with incumbent candidates are the more accurate, that hypothesis would be rejected. This suggests that with regard to poll accuracy, the effect of incumbency on the stability of voting preferences may be offset by the distorting influence that the high name recognition of incumbents has on preferences that are expressed in polls.

Another thread that runs through the above observations is that pre-election polls on low-visibility offices are relatively prone to error. Polling methodology has evolved in elections for high-visibility offices, such as the presidency. In such elections, media attention makes for high name recognition for all major party candidates by election day. Moreover, candidate identity may play a relatively minor role in voter decisions regarding low-visibility offices, so that question wordings that assume voters are choosing between individuals—which is the standard form used in pre-election polls—may not be appropriate. The fact is, as reported above, there is no consistent relation between office at stake and accuracy of pre-election polls.

OFF-YEAR, STATE, AND LOCAL ELECTIONS

Question wordings that are standard in pre-election polls (see Chapter 5) are based on the assumption that presenting each party's candidate for specified offices suffices to obtain a meaningful measurement of preference. While that assumption apparently is warranted for major offices, many of the pollsters personally inter-

viewed raised issues that challenge its validity with respect to low-visibility state and local offices. Also, a number of pollsters suggested that polling for such offices presents different problems in on-year and off-year elections. Nonetheless, there was little indication of much effort to develop alternative question wordings for low-visibility offices or to develop different measurement procedures for off-year and on-year elections.

The accuracy of pre-election polls on low-visibility offices reportedly varies according to whether high-visibility offices are at stake in the same election. Roberts's experience has been that pre-election polls on gubernatorial and senatorial elections are more accurate in on-year elections, when the presidency is also at stake, than in off-year elections. He speculates that this is because the presidential election sets the agenda for all races, making voters more conscious of the election and more likely to think seriously about how they will vote in all the races—not only for the presidency. Clymer concurs, observing that because of intensive media coverage, presidential elections capture more of the electorate's attention by one or two orders of magnitude. As a result, he maintains that voters "think harder about all the candidates and have more cogent reasons for deciding how to vote." If Roberts and Clymer are correct, expressions of voting preference between lesser-known candidates for lower-visibility offices would be more firmly fixed in on-year than in off-year elections.

Cole reports that in his experience elections for local office in off-years tend to be closer than are the results of pre-election polls on those races. He explains this in terms of the name-recognition advantage in polls that incumbents have over their challengers. He argues that off-year pre-election polls for low-visibility offices are distorted by this advantage since they do not adequately measure the effect of other influences, such as party identification, that come to play in the voting booth.

Coattail voting is another factor cited by some pollsters as influencing the accuracy of pre-election polls on races for low-visibility offices. Wetzel, for example, believes that polls on the 1984 primary in Indiana's First Congressional District were "distorted" by the concurrent presidential primary. In line with this interpretation, it would follow that if a pre-election poll on a low-visibility race in an on-year election did not first ask for presidential preference, it could be in serious error.

Teichner stresses both name recognition and turnout as factors that make for differences in pre-election poll accuracy in off-year and on-year elections for state and local offices. With respect to name recognition, his experience is that its effect on measured preference is greater in state and local elections than in presidential elections, while "mood" is more influential in presidential elections. He maintains that in on-year elections, expressions of voting preferences for all offices are likely to be channeled by an overarching mood, whereas in off-year elections they are more likely to be affected by whether any of the candidates are particularly well known. This position is very similar to that of Roberts and Clymer cited above.

With respect to the effect of turnout in off-year as compared with on-year elections, Teichner notes that there is greater variability in off-year turnout and that this variability significantly affects the results of elections for state and local office. He believes that in those elections last-minute swings in candidate strength may be more a matter of changes in the ability of candidates to activate their supporters to vote than a matter of changes in the proportion of the total voting-age population that prefers each candidate. Also, since turnout is greater when there is a presidential contest than when there isn't, a larger proportion of the electorate votes for low-visibility offices in on-year elections. This makes the accuracy of pre-election polls for state and local office particularly sensitive to how well the poll's methodology distinguishes correctly between likely voters and nonvoters. Consequently, the problems in properly identifying likely voters in low-turnout off-year elections, discussed earlier, make pre-election polls in such elections more prone to error.

Ferree adds the distinction between executive and legislative office. His experience is that elections for executive office, such as for the presidency or for state governor, are dominated by the electorate's "mood," a position very similar to Teichner's. Ferree maintains that, especially when an incumbent is running for reelection, executive elections are essentially referenda on performance in office. In comparison, he believes that elections for legislative office are more a matter of name recognition. Inferentially, the positioning of questions on such matters as approval of performance in office, important problems facing the state or nation, and familiarity with candidates' names might therefore have

different effects on pre-election poll accuracy, depending upon the office at stake.

Panagakis, Timberlake, and Kohut—all of whom have polled in Chicago elections—stress the effect of local political contexts upon poll accuracy. Panagakis claims that being able to vote a straight party ticket by recording a single vote rather than having to record a separate vote for each office is one important reason why polls in Chicago have been subject to serious error. Kohut concurs in that judgment and, as described in the preceding chapter, believes that in jurisdictions that provide for straight-ticket voting, it is necessary to ask a separate question regarding whether one intends to vote a straight ticket. Additionally, Timberlake says that the accuracy of pre-election polls conducted in environments dominated by machine wards, as is the case in Chicago, is adversely affected by respondent reluctance to give—even fear of giving—an honest answer in a poll. Consequently, he says it is especially difficult to determine the voting preferences of minority voters in Chicago.

Kohut summarizes his perspective on polling on local elections in the observations that "the actions of political organizations mediate the effect of institutions on behavior" and that "polls cannot measure the effect of institutions on individual behavior." He adds that local political context is less of an influence in national elections since variations in local context tend to cancel out, but in local elections they constitute a sometimes insuperable barrier to accuracy. If polls cannot measure institutional effects on individual behavior, this would constitute a devastating comment on the limits of the survey method's value to social science; a sophisticated social science must deal precisely with the interaction between institutional contexts and individual behavior. What is necessary is to specify hypothesized ways in which local political institutions mediate individual voting preferences and then seek to develop measures of those interactions.

For example, one mediating influence of political organizations is their efforts to mobilize their adherents to vote. Whether using measures of the success of political organizations in doing that— for example, considering the number of voters reached by telephone and door-do-door canvassers and the reach and recall of both direct mail and broadcast advertising—would add to the accuracy of local pre-election polls is a question that appears to be worth exploring.

Hart takes a position very different from those considered above in saying that polling on state and local elections can be easier than on national elections because sampling is easier in the former. His experience is that there are fewer "odd configurations of sampling points" in state and local elections that lead to measurement aberrations. (It seems likely that the incidence of "odd configurations" is more a matter of the number of sampling points in a state than whether a national or local election is involved.) Hart also notes that data from a greater number of prior elections are available for state and local elections for use in drawing and validating samples. Underlying the difference between Hart and the other pollsters is the contrast between a perspective that stresses sample design and one that emphasizes social psychological processes.

SALIENCY, INFORMATION LEVELS, AND CRYSTALLIZATION OF PREFERENCE

According to Zukin, because there are no network television channels in New Jersey, elections for major state offices have low visibility there as compared with other states. The result is that the recognition of the names of candidates for state and local offices— even incumbents—is particularly low. Zukin claims that because of these conditions, in New Jersey the impact of low saliency and information upon the accuracy of pre-election polls is especially evident. New Jersey voters become involved in state elections very late in a campaign, so that they often become informed about candidates and make up their minds during the final days before the election. Zukin believes that this explains why large, late swings in voting preferences for state contests are typical in New Jersey, whereas presidential elections are characterized by greater stability. For example, Zukin reports that the 1981 gubernatorial and 1982 senatorial elections were characterized by shifts in voter preference over the final campaign weekend that reversed previous candidate poll standings. He concludes that in New Jersey pre-election polls conducted as close as a week before an election for state office often miss the decisive campaign period and are, therefore, subject to considerable error.

Similar comments are made about polling on state offices in

California, a state that Zukin considers a "high information" state. Lewis reports that low awareness and late decision making are serious problems when polling on state and local elections in California. Also, his poll data indicate that about one-fourth of all Californians make up their minds during the final week of a campaign, a situation that creates a sizable potential for error in polls conducted before then.

What is common to both Zukin's and Lewis's observations is that elections characterized by low saliency and limited information are especially likely to be characterized by late decision making and crystallization of preference. But even high-saliency presidential elections are subject to late crystallization of preference— as, it is generally agreed, occurred in 1980. Even if they are salient and the electorate is well informed regarding them, late-crystallizing elections are especially difficult for pollsters. Not only are early expressions of preference poor indicators of ultimate voting behavior; even reasonably late pre-elections polls are subject to sizable error.

One indicator of crystallization mentioned by a number of pollsters is the strength of commitment to preferred candidates. In 1980, commitment to both Carter and Reagan was weak, and a large share of the electorate did not decide for whom to vote until the final days of the campaign. Roper found that 45% said their choice was based on who they thought was the worst of two poor choices, only one-third said they had voted for the presidency with enthusiasm, and one-fourth of the electorate made up their minds during the final week of the campaign. Similarly, Kohut reports that in the late-crystallizing 1980 election the Gallup Poll found that 45% were "very strong" in their preference for Reagan or Carter, compared with 65% who were "very strong" for Reagan or Mondale in the early-crystallizing 1984 election.

Kohut concludes that pre-election poll accuracy tends to be low in elections characterized by low commitment, so that he has limited "faith" in candidate poll standings when a high proportion of respondents do not express a firm commitment to their preferred candidate. Similarly, he recommends that measures of knowledge should be used as an indicator of the "hardness" of preference. Nonetheless, he says he knows of no way to factor measures of commitment and knowledge into a final estimate of candidates'

standing. That is, measures of commitment and knowledge can be used to estimate the potential for change in candidates' standing but cannot predict whether change will occur, nor in what direction.

LANDSLIDE ELECTIONS

Some pollsters have suggested that pre-election polls may be less likely to be accurate in landslide elections than in close elections. Garcia, for one, reports that his pre-election polls have been less accurate in landslide than in close elections. Similarly, Taylor says that pre-election polls tend to overestimate the magnitude of landslides. Pollsters who espouse this view think that to the extent polling error is greater in landslide elections, the error is due to a reduced turnout among the winning candidate's supporters— a reduction based on the expectation of a landslide.

The quantitative survey lends some support to the hypothesis that polling error is greater in landslide elections (see Table 6.3). Of the polls on elections in which the margin of victory was 6.4 points or less, 36% are in the high-accuracy tercile, compared with 29% of the polls on elections in which the margin of victory was greater. This difference approaches statistical significance in a two-tailed test and is significant in a one-tailed test. Since sampling error is greater for percentages near 50, one would predict that pre-election polls in landslide elections are the more accurate, making a one-tailed test appropriate. Mitofsky, however, idiosyncratically argues that one should think in terms of the number of votes rather than percentages and that then allowance for sampling error would be greater in landslide elections.

PRIMARIES AS LATE-CRYSTALLIZING ELECTIONS

Measuring voting preference in primary elections is widely described as a particularly difficult task. Taylor is typical in his comment that he has detected "incredible swings" in the final week of primary campaigns. Pollsters give a number of reasons explaining why pre-primary polls are especially prone to instability and error.

TABLE 6.3 / ACCURACY AND THE MARGIN OF VICTORY

	Margin of Victory	
Accuracy Tercile	Under 6.5% (%)	6.5% or more (%)
High	36	29
Medium	34	31
Low	30	40
Total	100	100
Number of polls	(278)	(142)

These reasons include low turnout and the absence of the stabilizing influence of party identification. After acknowledging the importance of these influences, Lewis nonetheless maintains that the biggest problem when polling on primaries is that voter preferences form late. Mitofsky agrees, emphasizing that primary campaigns are concentrated in the last four days, so that campaign effects go unmeasured by polls conducted earlier than that.

Both Black and Teichner attempt to explain the late crystallization of preference in primary campaigns by noting that knowledge of candidates in primary elections is often limited until those final days, when campaigning is concentrated. In the absence of knowledge, whatever preference may exist is tenuous and subject to rapid erosion. To illustrate this point, Black describes the 1982 New York Democratic gubernatorial primary, in which the seemingly invincible Koch was defeated in a late surge of Cuomo strength. He found that, initially, Jewish voters—a large voting bloc in the New York Democratic party—knew little about Cuomo other than that he is of Italian background whereas they knew that Koch is Jewish. At that stage of the campaign, according to Black, Koch was favored by about 85% of Jewish voters. As the campaign progressed, however, liberal Jewish voters became aware of Cuomo's ideological compatibility. Black reports that many Jewish voters then changed their preference, so that by September Koch commanded only half of the Jewish vote.

Teichner also warns of the risk of measuring preference in pri-

maries before the public's attention is focused on them, asserting that such polls get little more than "nonsense data." A case that he cites is the 1982 Republican senatorial primary in California. Early polls on that contest gave Barry Goldwater, Jr., a substantial, and apparently insurmountable, lead. In fact, Teichner says, those early polls were measuring little more than the familiarity of the Goldwater name. As the public became involved in the campaign and more knowledgeable about Goldwater's opponents, his early "lead" dissipated. Teichner warns that examining trends from early polls could create the impression that a candidate like Goldwater has lost a lead that he never really had.

The obvious inference from the above observations is that crystallization of preference, especially within the context of primaries, is often a transition from nonattitude to attitude. Pre-primary polls are a graphic illustration of how a sizable error can result if what are essentially nonattitudes are mistaken for real preference. While screening out nonvoters contributes significantly to the exclusion of nonattitudes from measures of candidate strength, it is still necessary to determine whether preference has crystallized among likely voters.

Since primaries are especially prone to be late-crystallizing elections, one would predict that pre-primary polls are subject to greater error than are polls in general elections. In the quantitative survey, 30% of pre-primary polls are in the high-accuracy tercile, compared with 35% of pre–general election polls (see Table 6.4). This difference is in the predicted direction and is at the borderline of significance using a one-tailed test. In evaluating the limited significance of the predicted difference, it should be remembered

TABLE 6.4 / ACCURACY AND THE TYPE OF ELECTION

Accuracy Tercile	General Election (%)	Primary (%)	Referendum (%)
High	35	30	14
Medium	33	30	57
Low	32	40	29
Total	100	100	100
Number of polls	(308)	(95)	(14)

that many general elections, especially at the state and local level, also crystallize late. For example, as DeBerge points out, political advertising in local elections is largely concentrated in the final days of the campaign, with voter involvement and commitment quite low until then. In contrast, presidential campaigns are typically in full swing weeks before the election.

REFERENDA

Referenda exemplify low-saliency, low-information elections in which campaigning is typically concentrated in the final few days before the election. Often poll respondents have little information about the issue other than what is provided in the wording of the poll question. As a result, poll measurements of voting preferences on referenda are, as Field puts it, "instructive" rather than a meaningful indicator of voting behavior. To cope with this problem, Lewis experimented with a three-step question sequence, first asking for an initial pro or con impression, then presenting arguments for and against the referendum, and finally asking for a voting preference—with little success.

Exacerbating the problems created by lack of information about the issue itself is, as Meyer points out, the nonpartisan nature of referenda, depriving voters of information about party alignment that might help them decide how to vote.

Tuchfarber has recorded complete reversals of opinion from midcampaign to election—in one case a shift as large as 50 points occurred in the final two weeks of a campaign. It is, therefore, not surprising that of the twenty-six polls on referenda that were identified in the quantitative survey, only 14% are in the high-accuracy tercile. The number of referenda is too small to determine whether there is a difference in accuracy when the turnout rate is controlled. Nonetheless, experience in polling on referenda drives home the lesson, applicable to all pre-election polls, that when a poll measures voting preferences based on limited knowledge and involvement, errors so gross as to render it meaningless as a predictor of voting behavior can be expected. In such instances, even a late poll can be completely misleading.

HIGH- VERSUS LOW-CRYSTALLIZED ELECTIONS

If the accuracy of a pre-election poll is contingent upon whether crystallization has occurred, an important polling task is to measure whether voter preferences have indeed crystallized. To do so requires a battery of questions that measure, for example, how salient an election has become to the electorate, the strength of belief systems that underlie preference, and the strength of commitment to the preferred candidate. If a pre-election poll indicates that crystallization has not as yet occurred, the candidates' standings as measured in that poll should be especially susceptible to change. However, whether change will take place, and the direction of any change, cannot be projected from the existence of that susceptibility. Thus, pollsters who measure these aspects of preference report that in their experience such measures are useful for "diagnostic" or analytical purposes and not for improving accuracy.

Measures of crystallization could be used to classify elections according to their potential for change. Presumably, the total expected accuracy band—that is, the combination of sampling and nonsampling errors—would be larger for low-crystallized than for high-crystallized elections. This is different from the frequently used caveat that "the undecided will determine the election." Such caveats are often little more than journalistic escape hatches. Rather, what is suggested is the hypothesis that polls with low-crystallization scores would be, on the average, less accurate than polls with high-crystallization scores. If this hypothesis were confirmed, it would provide a sounder base for evaluating the accuracy of pre-election polls than now exists.

7 / Stability and Lability of Voting Preferences

Two central issues in any evaluation of poll methodology are (1) whether it is possible to identify a time frame within which pre-election polls must be conducted in order to achieve an acceptable level of predictive power, and (2) whether special research designs are needed if polls conducted within an appropriate time frame are to have predictive value.

The pollsters who were personally interviewed agreed that since polls measure candidates' standing as it exists at the time of interviewing, pre-election polls can be very misleading if voting preferences change between the end of interviewing and election day. (It is for this reason that in this study only the results of "final" pre-election polls have been considered.) This understanding of what it is that polls measure dates back to the 1948 Truman-Dewey election, when, during the final month of the campaign, Truman overcame an early, apparently decisive Dewey lead. Since then, many pollsters have endeavored to develop methods for determining whether there are changes in voting preferences taking place that would affect the election outcome and what the size of that effect would be. Some claim to have achieved considerable

success in their endeavors, while others have concluded that the electoral process is too unstable for polls to achieve such a goal.

CLOSENESS OF PRE-ELECTION POLLS TO ELECTIONS

The occurrence of last-minute shifts is often given as a major reason for discrepancies between poll results and election outcome. Mitofsky and Kohut, for example, report that post-election analyses in 1980 show that a last-minute swing to Reagan changed an election "too close to call" into a decisive victory. Similarly, Sussman and Hart report that their polls picked up a strong trend from Mondale to Gary Hart at the very end of the 1984 New Hampshire Democratic primary campaign, a trend that was missed by pollsters who did not continue polling through the final pre-primary weekend.

Despite concern with last-minute trends, only a minority of the polls in the quantitative survey were conducted in the closing days of their respective election campaigns (see Table 7.1). Interviewing was completed for 25% of the polls within five days of the election, for 44% of the polls within six to twelve days, and for 31% of the polls within thirteen days or more. The expectation that the closer to the election a poll is conducted, the greater the likelihood that poll results will correspond to election outcome is confirmed by the quantitative survey. The zero order correlation between poll accuracy and the number of days between interviewing and the election is a statistically significant .21. Also, in two

TABLE 7.1 / TIMING OF POLL INTERVIEWING

		Accuracy Tercile		
Length of Time before Election	All Polls (%)	High (%)	Medium (%)	Low (%)
1–5 days	25	34	26	14
6–12 days	44	44	43	45
13 days or more	31	22	31	41
Total	100	100	100	100
Number of polls	(430)	(140)	(140)	(140)

TABLE 7.2 / ACCURACY AND TIMING OF INTERVIEWING

Accuracy Tercile	Length of Time between Interview and Election		
	Less Than 5 Days (%)	5–12 Days (%)	More Than 12 Days (%)
High	45	34	24
Medium	36	32	33
Low	19	34	43
Total	100	100	100
Number of polls	(104)	(185)	(131)

regression models that were tested, the beta value for the variable "number of days between the election and interviewing" (.20) is the largest obtained for any of the independent variables (see Table 9.2). Furthermore, only if interviewing is conducted within days of the election is there a strong likelihood that a poll will provide an accurate measure of voting behavior: of the polls that were completed within five days of the election, 45% were in the high-accuracy tercile. This compares with 34% of polls completed within six to twelve days of the election and 24% of those completed before that (see Table 7.2).

The fact that of the polls conducted two weeks or more before election day, about one-fourth are within the high-accuracy tercile may mislead some to assume that there is no inherent methodological weakness in early polls. Citing the apparant accuracy of some early polls, however, ignores the variability between elections in terms of how and when voting preferences crystallize.

The significant correlation between accuracy and the closeness of interviewing to the election explains the importance most pollsters place on interviewing for pre-election polls within very short time spans. Common practice is to allow three to five days at most for interviewing—even with samples of 1,500 or more. Measures of voting preferences aggregated over longer periods of time, it was generally agreed, will mask any significant shifts that may be occurring. Link notes that when the *Daily News* Straw Poll aggregated interviews that were conducted over a month-long pe-

riod, it had a very poor accuracy record. In 1968, the interviewing schedule for this poll was changed to three waves of four days each. Link reports that the accuracy of the final poll, completed immediately before election day, was far superior to previous experience.

DIFFERENCES IN THE "CHRONOLOGY" OF ELECTIONS

A number of processes underlie the correlation between accuracy and the length of the time between interviewing and election day. These relate to (1) how far in advance of an election voters first make up their minds, (2) how firm those decisions are, and (3) the occurrence of major events during the election campaign. If voters make firm decisions early in the campaign, even major events may have limited impact. In such elections, early polls can be deceptively accurate. But it is apparent from the quantitative survey data that in most elections enough voters are sufficiently uncertain in their initial preferences, or else enough do not reach a decision until late in a campaign, so that early polls are subject to sizable error.

Teeter cautions that not only do early polls measure preferences that are subject to change, but they often attempt to measure preferences that have yet to come into existence. What may appear to be a volatile electorate, continually changing its mind as to which candidate it prefers, may, in reality, be an electorate in the process of learning who the candidates are and what they are like. In a similar vein, Roper severely criticizes early polls, claiming they measure little more than name recognition and not voting preference.

The timing of a series of polls in relation to campaigning and other events can affect trend measurements. In 1984, polls conducted by ABC News/*Washington Post*, CBS News/*New York Times*, and Harris each indicated temporary gains of up to 4 points for Mondale in the wake of his first debate with Reagan, while polls conducted by NBC News, the *Los Angeles Times*, and Black (for *USA Today*) did not. Black interprets this difference as a consequence of timing. He observes that the former three polls were conducted immediately after the debate, whereas the latter three

were conducted slightly later. He infers that some Democrats who favored Reagan had initially shifted away from him immediately after the debate but then drifted back within a few days.

Since the measured volatility of an election can be affected by the timing of interviewing, caution must be exercised in ascribing polling error to voter volatility. Nonetheless, variations between elections in the susceptibility of voters to change is cited by pollsters as a reason why some elections are more difficult for them than others. Black is typical in claiming that the 1984 presidential election was characterized by an "early decision cycle" and that Reagan's vote was "harder" in 1984 than in 1980. Field agrees that voters' intentions in the 1984 presidential campaign were stable. He also observes that there were few significant events that could have influenced voter preferences in 1984, in contrast to the highly charged political atmosphere of 1980.

One might expect that in light of the early closure, or crystallization, of voting preferences, the 1984 election is one in which pre-election poll accuracy would be high. In fact, although there was general agreement that Reagan would win by a comfortable majority, there were sizable differences among polls in their final measurements of the size of Reagan's projected victory—with a low estimate of 55%–45% from Roper to a high estimate of 60%–35% (with 5% undecided) from Black. This range is greater than the fluctuations in voting preferences that Gallup measured over the final month of the campaign (*Gallup Report* 1984). Although the "volatility" of a campaign may affect to some degree the ability of pre-election polls to provide an accurate indication of how the electorate will vote, volatility clearly does not explain the highly variable 1984 performance of pre-election polls. Volatility undoubtedly makes accuracy more difficult to achieve, but stability does not ensure it.

Problems in Conducting Polls Close to Election Day

If, to achieve accuracy, a poll is conducted very close to the election, a very fast data processing and analysis schedule must be adhered to so that the poll results may be reported in time to meet journalistic needs. The resultant time pressures constitute a seri-

ous problem for poll accuracy. Unless all the details involved in designing and implementing a poll have been carefully laid out, polls conducted under the pressure of tight time schedules can easily get out of control. This pressure is especially stringent for magazines, somewhat less so for newspapers, and least for television. In addition, personal interview polls require more time than do telephone polls, and use of the former technique may further aggravate tight time schedules.

Illustrative of the special efforts that may be needed to meet the twin needs of polling as close to an election as possible and reporting the results before election day is the procedure that Perry devised for analyzing the final pre-election Gallup Poll, conducted by personal interview days before the election. In 1950, it had been decided to conduct two polls, one four weeks before the election and the second the week immediately preceding election day, using the same areal units (election precincts) for each. This was intended to provide the basis for the latest possible trend measurement. In 1952, to estimate that trend, Perry analyzed the results of the first poll in two ways—using a full estimating procedure and by means of a truncated procedure based on aggregations of each interviewer's assignments. For the second poll, each interviewer hand-tallied his or her assignment to correspond to the truncated method that had been applied to the first survey. These hand tallies were telegraphed (in later years, telephoned) to the Gallup office. The trend between the two surveys as measured by the truncated procedure was then applied to the results of the first survey based on the complete estimation model. By the 1960s, this procedure enabled Gallup to conduct its final national poll, based on over 5,000 personal interviews, on the Thursday, Friday, and Saturday before election day and still wire poll results to its newspaper clients by Sunday noon.

While Perry believes this procedure for conducting polls up to the last few days of a campaign has contributed to Gallup Poll accuracy, he also points out that it is vulnerable to measurement error at the analysis stage. After each election, when all the individual questionnaires from the second poll were data entered, he analyzed them using his full estimation model. Those analyses produced estimates of candidate strength that were consistently

more accurate than the initial estimates. For example, Perry reports that in 1980 a postelection analysis applying the full estimation model to the complete data base for the second survey appreciably reduced the published 3.8 percentage point underestimate of Reagan's vote. He thinks three reasons account for the difference: (1) there are errors in the interviewers' hand tallies, (2) the use of aggregated data increases variance, and (3) there is error in estimating the trend by means of the truncated method. In recent elections, therefore, instead of tallying their results and telephoning the aggregated data, interviewers have telephoned their results respondent by respondent. (Roper, who also conducts personal interview national polls, has experimented with interviewers telephoning in their hand tallies and has also found that procedure to be less accurate than having respondent-by-respondent responses telephoned in.)

Telephone polls do not have the problem of physically transporting completed questionnaires from distant interviewers to a central data entry facility. But organizations that conduct telephone polls must still enter the results and analyze them under severe time constraints. The television networks have devoted considerable resources to dealing with this problem. ABC News/ *Washington Post* and NBC News rely upon CATI (computer assisted telephone interviewing) systems in which interviewers enter responses directly into a computer (i.e., into disk storage) as they conduct their interviews, thereby eliminating the need for a separate, and time-consuming, data entry stage. The CBS News/ *New York Times* Poll does not use a CATI system, but it has developed procedures for the almost instantaneous transport of hard copy questionnaires to a data entry facility, so that there is a minimal time lag between completion of interviewing and availability of the data for analysis. All three television networks have developed tabulation programs that give their analysts immediate, direct access to the data. As a result, their polls can be ready to report candidate standing based on their final pre-election polls within just a few hours of completing their interviews. Polls that have not developed professional fast turnaround procedures have to accept a time lag of days between the completion of interviewing and the time when analyzed data become available—a situation that can decrease poll accuracy if there is a last-minute trend

in voting preferences—or else they must "make do" with limited quality controls—a situation that will add to total survey error.

Measuring Last-Minute Trends

Some polling organizations base their final estimate of voting preferences on designs that require the measurement of trends from a baseline survey. (The Gallup method described above is illustrative.) It is, therefore, pertinent to note that in 1964, when Goldwater ran against Johnson for president, the final published Gallup and Harris poll results were identical. However, the Gallup report indicated that there had been a small increase in Goldwater's strength from its previous poll, while the Harris report indicated a small decrease. Thus, while the two polls were equally accurate as indicators of the election outcome, they were in conflict with regard to what the trend had been during the closing weeks of the campaign. The question, arises, therefore, as to what kind of a survey design will provide the best measure of last-minute trends.

In the absence of a tested design for measuring trends, pollsters are forced to rely on judgment. In the 1984 Honolulu mayoralty election, Dannemiller reports that three successive polls charted a trend from the incumbent to the challenger, with the final poll showing a "dead heat." A straight-line projection "would have given the nod to him [the challenger]." Dannemiller concluded that the straight line could not be believed and used an adjustment based on what was known about turnout. The turnout adjustment incorrectly indicated that the incumbent would win.

Three types of sample designs for measuring last-minute trends were described in the personal interviews as currently in use, with considerable disagreement as to their comparative value. These designs involve (1) two or more surveys, each based on an independent sample, (2) "rolling samples" that track trends day by day, and (3) panels. They are described below.

Independent samples. Conducting two or more surveys using independent samples is the simplest and most conventional design. Peter Hart reports that in the 1984 New Hampshire Democratic primary campaign he conducted three successive polls, each based on samples of about 500–600 cases. These polls identified a

clear trend toward Gary Hart—from 10% on the first poll to 17% on the second and 22% on the third. A trend of that magnitude is statistically significant with the sample sizes that were used. However, with a less marked shift in voter preferences, appreciably larger samples would have to be used before one could say with confidence that there had been a real change. And, it will be remembered that about one-fourth of the polls in the quantitative survey were based on samples of fewer than 400 (see page 62).

To minimize the possibility that an apparent change is nothing more than random error, some pollsters use replicated sample designs (that is, samples comprised of two or more parts, each of which is by itself a complete sample). Zukin has used a split-sample design for his final poll, with one replicate interviewed during the first three days of interviewing and the second during the final three days. This yields an empirical variance estimate that provides a check on the possibility that a last-minute change in voting preferences may be occurring.

Similarly, Kohut reports that in state polls conducted by Gallup in 1984, interviewing was spread over four days, with a different replicate used each day. Each day's sample was weighted to match all the replicates demographically. The returns from the first two days of interviewing were compared with those from the latter two days to evaluate whether any shift in voter preference had occurred. According to Kohut, this method gives the "context" of the final days of the campaign even though the small daily samples are insufficient to yield a precise measure of change. Thus, in the 1984 Illinois senatorial election, this method identified a "softness" in Percy's vote and a presumptive movement toward Simon. The published poll result was based on the four-day composite, with the indication of a trend toward Simon taken into account.

Even when sample replicates are used, it can be difficult to differentiate between random variability and real change in voting preference. This is shown in the experience of the Harris Survey in the 1968 and 1980 presidential elections. Taylor reports that in 1968 three replicates of 1,000 each were drawn for the final Harris pre-election poll. Interviewing was conducted on three successive days, with a different replicate used each day. There was an apparent trend toward Humphrey over those three days, with Hum-

phrey narrowly leading Nixon on the last day. Accepting that trend as real, Harris published the last day's results. If the three-day composite had been used, Taylor reports, it would have correctly pointed to a narrow Nixon victory. On the other hand, when a similar sample design was used in 1980, in a postelection analysis the results of the final day's interviewing were a more accurate indicator of the size of Reagan's victory over Carter than was the three-day composite.

When using sample designs such as Taylor describes, the analyst may choose between (1) relying on judgment to decide whether there is a real trend—always a risky procedure—or (2) applying variance estimates, such as Zukin describes, to assess the likelihood that changes are real and not random fluctuations.

Rolling samples. The use of replicated sample designs on successive days has been expanded by some pollsters into what has come to be called "rolling samples." Statistically, rolling samples are no more than an averaging of a series of small independent samples. Their unique feature is that there is no time gap between each interviewing wave, with a moving average of successive waves calculated to smooth random fluctuations. Adherents claim that this produces a valid trend measurement.

The ABC News/*Washington Post* polls have used a design in which replicates of 500 are interviewed on successive nights. Callbacks are made to one night's not-at-homes on the following night (a procedure that the Census Bureau pioneered). Alderman reports that to protect against misinterpreting random fluctuation for trend, a rolling average is used rather than comparing daily results. Sussman, in expressing satisfaction with the rolling sample, reported that in the 1984 presidential election it picked up a small last-minute gain for Mondale.

Teeter cautions against relying on interviewing over a few days in order to measure trends, even when replicated sample designs are used. He contends that month-long tracking studies are needed to differentiate "blips" from true trends. In his private polling, Teeter has scheduled interviewing over extended periods using relatively small daily replicates and then calculated rolling averages to smooth out random fluctuations. Teeter's procedure differs from that used by ABC News/*Washington Post* in that it is designed to measure trends over the course of a campaign,

whereas the latter focuses on what may be happening in the final few days. This contrast in time perspective is less a methodological disagreement than a reflection of the different concerns of the private pollster and the media pollster, with the former seeking to chart persisting movements and the latter seeking to obtain time-bound measurements of voter preferences.

A number of pollsters question the methodological soundness of rolling samples for measuring trends. One source of criticism is concern about the relatively small daily samples that are used, making short-term movements suspect even after averaging. Lewis, for example, avoids rolling samples, calling them "dangerous" in that the small daily samples produce "sloppy" data. An additional concern is that the random fluctuation that remains in small rolling samples even after averaging can create a distorted picture of what is happening within a short time period. Black fears that rolling samples are subject to big blips even after averaging and, consequently, are apt to show more movement in voter preferences than do independent samples.

The criticisms of rolling samples voiced by Lewis and Black are most applicable to their use for measuring short-term trends, for example, in the final few days before an election. Without very large daily samples and stringent controls, the possibility that normal fluctuations would spuriously create the appearance of a trend cannot be discounted. In the absence of strong evidence that voter preferences are changing over night in reaction to an event of extraordinary impact, a three- or four-day composite would appear to be superior to a two-day moving average of small samples. The value of rolling samples appears to be greatest for charting long-term trends, in which blips can be identified against the background of any overall movement of preference.

Panels. Sussman reports that panels identified last-minute trends in the 1981 Virginia gubernatorial and the 1982 District of Columbia mayoralty elections, as well as a small change in the closing days of the 1984 presidential election. Similarly, Zukin reports that his use of panels correctly detected late swings to Kean in the 1981 New Jersey gubernatorial election and to Lautenberg in the 1982 New Jersey senatorial election.

Zukin cited as an advantage of panels over independent surveys for measuring changes in voting preference that there is no

sampling error in panel measures of change on the individual level. This eliminates the problem of interpreting small net movements in voting preference. He notes that a 3-point difference between two independent polls is a tenuous base for concluding that voting preferences have changed. He has used panel data to test the reality of trends as measured by successive independent polls and claims that this has enabled him to detect the trends noted above, which he believes he would have missed had he relied only upon independent samples.

There is general agreement among users and nonusers of panels that the method provides a valuable tool for analyzing individual switching of voting preferences. Sussman, a user, says that a special value of panels for him is that they detect switching even when marginals remain unchanged. Clymer, a nonuser, rates panels as superior to asking retrospective "why" questions in independent polls for the analysis of switching behavior. Nonetheless, many pollsters who accept the analytic value of panels still expressed concern that they yield biased measures of trend. Traugott, who has used panels to analyze "election dynamics," says that since independent samples measure net change (even if one is limited to inference when using them for analyzing election dynamics), he would rely upon that type of design for the most accurate final pre-election measurement. He also believes that rolling samples are good for spotting trend directions.

Black is typical of many nonusers in pointing to panel effect (the sensitizing of respondents to the election) and to sample attrition as sources of bias that are inherent in the panel method. Mitofsky takes a different position concerning sample attrition but agrees with respect to panel effect. He notes that if the base survey for a panel is of high quality and proper adjustments are made for sample attrition, sample bias need not be a serious problem. However, he would still be worried about panel effects. Lewis concedes that in principle panels are the best way to measure trends, but he is concerned that the complex weighting procedures needed to compensate for sample attrition are a source of error in their own right.

At least some pollsters who use panels have applied the kind of weighting procedures to control for possible bias resulting from sample attrition that Mitofsky notes is essential. Sussman and

Hagan report that the ABC News/*Washington Post* Poll uses the following procedure to weight the sample from the second interviewing wave to fit the baseline survey: Respondents to the second wave are first classified by their candidate preference on the baseline survey. Then, using a ratio adjustment procedure, each grouping of second-wave respondents is weighted back to the demographic profile of all baseline respondents who preferred that candidate. A thirty-six cell matrix of sex, age, race, and education values is used for this purpose. (It should be noted that only registered voters are reinterviewed, and the weighting process is based on the demographic characteristics of registered voters in the baseline survey.)

Zukin also weights second-wave respondents back to the baseline survey, but by a somewhat different procedure. Using the baseline data, he creates a seven-point scale—Firm Democratic, Soft Democratic, Undecided Democratic, Undecided, Undecided Republican, Soft Republican, Firm Republican. Second-wave respondents are classified according to these categories and then weighted demographically to fit the profiles of all baseline respondents in their respective categories.

Traugott, in an analysis of the characteristics of respondents to baseline surveys who are not successfully reinterviewed, found that these respondents are disproportionately uninterested in the election. Also, in 1984, those successfully reinterviewed were disproportionately for Reagan. This suggests that attrition bias is a problem primarily among those less likely to vote and, at least in runaway elections, among adherents of the trailing candidate. Another interpretation is based on the correlation between voting behavior and socioeconomic status: since adults of high socioeconomic status were especially prone to vote, and to vote for Reagan, this may explain Traugott's findings.

To limit the sensitizing of respondents, Sussman does not inform them that they will be reinterviewed. Also, he reinterviews them only once. Comparable procedures are used by Zukin and Traugott. Nonetheless, Traugott reports that he has detected a small panel effect (including an increased level of interest among those successfully reinterviewed) for which he has not been able to develop any corrective procedure. It seems likely, therefore, that even if sample bias were eliminated by the weighting proce-

dures described above, some residual panel effect bias would still exist. For that reason, panel measures of changing preferences cannot be considered precise measurements of change, however useful they may be for developing general estimates of change.

In fact, Sussman and Zukin indicate that they do not rely on their panel data to form precise estimates of change. Despite his commitment to the panel method, Sussman does not rely exclusively upon panel data for measuring trends but uses them in conjunction with a "tracking" (rolling) sample that is conducted in parallel with the panel. Zukin uses a more elaborate, though economical, procedure for relating panel data to independent polls. He conducts a series of interviewing waves, with successive waves consisting of a new independent sample plus reinterviews with a subsample of respondents from the previous wave's independent sample. The reinterviews are conducted with (1) all "soft" voters, that is, those who say they might change their minds, plus (2) a subsample of "hard" voters, that is, those who are committed and are sure of their preference. This concentrates Zukin's resources on those most prone to change without neglecting the possibility that some apparently committed voters might also switch. He uses change as measured by the panel to evaluate differences between successive independent samples.

COMPARISON OF THE THREE DESIGNS FOR MEASURING LAST-MINUTE TRENDS

The fact that poll accuracy increases with closeness of interviewing to election day emphasizes the importance of late changes in voter preference to the accuracy of pre-election polls. Being able to determine whether any changes are occurring, their direction, and their strength would add to the value of even last-minute polls for projecting the likely vote in an election. Independent samples, rolling samples, and panels have all been used for this purpose. Each method has its value, but each also has its limitations.

Rolling samples based on interviewing small replicates on a daily basis appear to be of least value for measuring movement in candidates' standing during the last few days of a campaign. Their

value is more in charting the overall course of a campaign than in measuring what is happening within a few days. Panels are attractive because they can be used to analyze campaign dynamics as well as to estimate trends; but even with sophisticated controls that correct for sample attrition bias, they are not precision instruments for measuring last-minute trends. Used in conjunction with other techniques, however, they can be very useful.

Charting the change from an earlier poll to a last-minute poll, each based on an independent sample, does not provide grounds for projecting what changes may be occurring subsequent to the completion of interviewing. In combination with panel data, however, this method can provide a valid assessment of the likely direction of last-minute changes—even though precise estimates of the magnitude of change may not be possible.

Last-minute polls based on independent samples have to be scheduled over a number of days in order to interview an adequately large sample. The use of replicated sample designs that facilitate the estimation of variances over the interviewing period during which a last-minute poll is conducted, which might be considered a special application of the rolling sample, appears to be a useful design. There is a danger in this design, however, that normal random daily fluctuations will be mistaken for true change. Estimates of the statistical significance of daily differences are needed, preferably in conjunction with confirmatory data from other sources, for example, panels.

8 / Characteristics of Polling Organizations

Pre-election polls are conducted under sharply different operating conditions that can significantly affect their accuracy. The conditions differ first with respect to the importance given to achieving accurate election predictions. They differ second with respect to organizational structure, namely, the type of professional staff that designs and analyzes the polls, the type of interviewing staff that is employed, and whether interviewing is conducted at a central telephone location.

ACCURACY AS A GOAL OF PRE-ELECTION POLLS

Accurately "predicting" election outcome is not an important goal for many pollsters (see Table 8.1). Some have as their explicit policy the avoidance of any basis for treating their polls "as a forecast of events to come." For example, in order that their polls not be treated as predictions, Rappeport, Lewis, and Merrill will not conduct pre-election polls in the final week before an election. Similarly, Field has issued numerous public statements distin-

guishing between survey results as factual representations of reality at a given time and predictions as interpretations of survey results. Others, like Perry, agree that a pre-election poll is a measurement of preference at the time it is conducted but, nonetheless, accept the closeness of their polls conducted in the final week of a campaign to election results as a valid criterion for evaluating the accuracy and quality of their methodology.

The rejection of the accurate prediction of elections as a polling objective is based on a number of considerations. These include expediency, public policy, concern about public ignorance of sampling error, and doubts as to the scientific meaningfulness of treating polls as predictions. The importance of each of these considerations to individual pollsters varies, with many influenced by more than one.

In the personal interviews, a number of pollsters commented that if only for reasons of sampling error, consistent accuracy is not a meaningful objective of pre-election polls. Since some "error" must always be expected, there is always the possibility that a well-designed and well-implemented poll will be "wrong" in a given election. Not conducting a "final," presumptively predictive poll is a practical way of avoiding that possibility. Typically, this attitude is bolstered by other reasons for not conducting final polls that the public will perceive as predictions.

Lewis avoids publishing a final poll on the grounds that it would make no contribution to the newspaper or to the public. To him, achieving a high level of accuracy is always problematic, and he sees "no reason to put the newspaper's reputation for accuracy on the line in a crap shoot." His position is that polls cannot predict the future, but they can provide important insights about "today," and it is those insights that are his primary objectives. A special value of pre-election polls for him is that they help reporters do a better job of covering an election. Instead of being dependent on leaked private polls, reporters can rely on objective media-sponsored polls. Wetzel takes a similar position, noting that a major function of the pre-election polls conducted by NBC News is to educate the news staff about the election, and they are not meant to produce a prediction. By way of illustration, he reports that an analysis of the "internals" of the 1984 NBC polls indicated that Reagan's strength was "strong" but that evidence

of conflict among Mondale's supporters implied that the latter's real voting strength was overstated. This analysis was provided to the NBC news staff as an aid to their interpretation of election results.

Merrill gives two reasons for not polling in the final week of a campaign—to protect the poll's reputation in the event that a final poll deviates appreciably from the election, and in order to avoid the possibility that publication of poll results might influence the election. Rappeport used to conduct final polls but says he has discontinued that practice because he now feels that "analysis" rather than prediction is the proper role of polls. Alderman also says analysis is his primary goal, but he does not refuse to conduct a final poll for that reason. Neither does he make a high degree of accuracy of his final polls a major goal. He feels that "it is good enough" if poll results are reasonably close to an election's outcome, even if they are not "precisely right." If reasonable accuracy is achieved, he maintains, one can still explain the election, analyzing who is for whom and why.

Field is highly critical of those who use close correspondence of poll findings to election results as a criterion of poll accuracy. He maintains that the only acceptable criterion is the soundness of the poll's design and methodology, for example, the use of probability sampling. Furthermore, he views voting as a unique type of event: the act of voting occurs within a very narrow time frame and, therefore, is an activity unrelated to anything else measured by surveys. For that reason, he rejects Gallup's often cited contention that pre-election polls provide an acid test of the validity of the survey method.

Field also argues that in order to predict an election, one has to use poll data in conjunction with judgment based on other, often qualitative data. To support this view, he referred to a remark of William Roberts, the political consultant, regarding the 1982 California gubernatorial election. Roberts had felt that 5 points should be deducted from Bradley's strength in the pre-election polls to adjust for antiblack prejudice. With respect to the 1980 presidential election, Field reports that in midcampaign, when national polls were reporting Carter slightly ahead of Reagan, he had given a talk in which he observed that on the basis of a number of state polls that had Reagan ahead, one might well

predict a Reagan victory. Prediction, he concludes, has to be based on analyzing available data from all polls rather than on a projection from only one.

Timberlake reports that two polling approaches were considered by the *Chicago Tribune*—a "horse race" poll based on interviews with a 1,000-case sample, and an "issues" approach based on 500 interviews. The issues approach was adopted for three reasons: (1) the superficiality and short shelf life of horse-race polls, (2) their comparability with the results from polls conducted outside the context of election campaigns, and (3) their comparative cheapness.

A frequent comment of pollsters in the qualitative survey was that every election is so different that—as Timberlake put it—a different model may be needed for each election. Timberlake adds that pre-election polling is not a predictive science, so one cannot expect to predict an election within the sampling error allowance of 3–4 points for typical sample sizes. Drawing an analogy with marketing research, he asserts that just as consumer surveys cannot predict the number of cars that will be sold though they can identify the types of consumers who buy foreign or domestic cars, pre-election polls cannot predict election outcome even though they can provide the basis for analyzing an election.

Wetzel also has reservations about the scientific rigor of poll methodology, but from a somewhat different perspective. He cautions that it is necessary to understand "the fragility of the data," that one should recognize that each election is a different event, so that imposing one's logic on variable behavior is not warranted. Similarly, Link describes polling as a "soft technique" that requires a high degree of interaction between the analyst and his or her data base. Variation in analytic methods can lead to different conclusions being drawn from comparable, or even identical, data bases.

A statistical "experiment" of Zukin's is pertinent to Link's observations. In seeking to understand why his and another poll reported different candidate standings on the same race, Zukin was able to reproduce the standings of the other poll by applying its method for identifying likely voters (based on unaided candidate name awareness) to his data. Zukin reports that using the other poll's method on his own data virtually duplicated the other

poll's results, which were less accurate than those produced by his method. As this exercise illustrates, the fact that variations in methodology lead to different projections of candidate standing does not mean that each variation is equally sound. Zukin concludes that although each election is different, there is a need to develop expertise over many elections by continually testing alternative methods. In this, he takes a position similar to that of Perry and other pollsters for whom accuracy is an important goal. Although agreeing that each election does present a unique challenge, Perry stresses the need to develop a standardized methodology, as he did in developing his turnout scale, with provision for modifications that adjust the method to changing conditions. He maintains that acknowledging the uniqueness of each election does not *a fortiori* lead to the conclusions that each election must be treated as a singular event so that a different measurement and analysis model must be developed for each.

Mitofsky is also in sharp disagreement with pollsters who reject poll accuracy as a meaningful criterion for assessing the quality of pre-election polls. He maintains that the poor accuracy record of many polls results from the use of inferior and sloppy research methods, for example, the use of nonprobability sample designs and poorly thought out, *ad hoc* estimation procedures. His position is that if sound methodology were employed, the magnitude of deviation between final pre-election polls and election results would be significantly reduced. In this context, it is noteworthy that Teeter, a private pollster normally under great pressure to conduct economic, fast turnaround polls, reports that he periodically conducts very careful polls utilizing full probability samples. He uses their results to evaluate the results from his other polls. Implicit in this practice is the assumption that with proper methods and adequate resources, the accuracy of pre-election polls could be improved.

It would be incorrect, and grossly unfair, to infer that all pollsters for whom predictive accuracy (in the sense of closeness of final candidate standings to election results) is not an important criterion are unconcerned with the quality and soundness of their research designs. To the contrary, many devote considerable resources to their sample designs, interviewing methods, and analytic procedures. As a result, some of them have in fact achieved

TABLE 8.1 / IMPORTANCE OF POLL ACCURACY

"Is a highly accurate prediction of elections an important criterion when evaluating the success of your pre-election polls?"

	All Polls (%)	High (%)	Medium (%)	Low (%)
			Accuracy Tercile	
Extremely important	35	43	31	29
Important	43	39	48	44
Not too important	16	11	18	18
Not at all important	6	7	3	9
Total	100	100	100	100
Number of polls	(338)	(114)	(113)	(103)

good accuracy records. Nonetheless, a reasonable hypothesis is that the emphasis they put on "analysis" as opposed to "prediction," coupled with the practice of not conducting polls in the final days of a campaign, would result in their polls being subject to greater error than polls conducted by those who stress accuracy.

This hypothesis is supported by data from the quantitative survey, which show that 43% of the polls conducted by organizations for whom predictive accuracy is "an extremely important criterion for evaluating the success of your pre-election polls" are in the high-accuracy tercile (see Table 8.2). Of the polls conducted by organizations for whom accuracy is "important" (but not "extremely important"), 31% are in the high-accuracy tercile, as are 29% of those for whom accuracy is "not too" or "not at all" important (see Table 8.2). It is impossible to determine from these data how much of this significant difference is caused by a diversion of attention and resources away from accuracy by those less interested in accuracy, and how much by a rejection of accuracy as a goal among those who have been unsuccessful in their attempts to achieve high accuracy. However, it is the case that those who do stress accuracy have been most successful in this regard.

This study does not deal with policy reasons for not conducting final pre-election polls that are intended to act as reliable indicators of election outcome. It may indeed be foolish for a newspaper or television station to risk its reputation for accuracy by con-

TABLE 8.2 / ACCURACY AND THE IMPORTANCE OF ACCURACY

Accuracy Tercile	Extremely Important (%)	Less Than Extremely Important		
		All (%)	Important (%)	Not Too/Not At All Important (%)
High	43	30	31	29
Medium	31	36	38	33
Low	26	34	31	38
Total	100	100	100	100
Number of polls	(114)	(216)	(143)	(73)

ducting such polls. And it may indeed serve the public interest more to focus on analysis instead of prediction. But the fact that those for whom accuracy is extremely important tend to be more accurate does demonstrate that there are ways of improving the accuracy of pre-election polls.

ORGANIZATIONAL STRUCTURE

Of the polls covered in the quantitative survey, 40% were designed and analyzed by "professional researchers who are on a paper's or station's staff" and 9% by "newspaper or station staff." (The distinction between these two categories is not as sharp as one might assume. For example, in many instances the professional researchers have marketing research as their primary responsibility and have little background in public opinion and election research. On the other hand, there are some political reporters who have specialized in polling and have become quite knowledgeable about survey methodology.) An additional 22% of the polls were designed and analyzed by independent survey research firms, 16% by a combination of staff researcher and outside consultant, 2% by an outside consultant only, and 12% had other arrangements (a few reported using more than one arrangement) (see Table 8.3).

The polls that were designed and analyzed by independent

TABLE 8.3 / WHO DESIGNS AND ANALYZES POLLS

Poll Analysts	All Polls (%)	Accuracy Tercile		
		High (%)	Medium (%)	Low (%)
Newspaper or station staff	9	10	9	7
Professional researchers on paper's or station's staff	40	31	44	43
An outside consultant	2	2	2	4
Both staff researchers and outside consultant	16	17	16	14
An outside survey research firm	22	29	18	17
Other	16	10	11	15
Total	105*	99*	100	100
Number of polls	(372)	(127)	(126)	(110)

*Totals do not add up to 100% because of rounding.

survey research firms are significantly more likely to be accurate than are those that were handled by professional staff researchers (see Table 8.4). Of the former, 47% are in the high-accuracy tercile as compared with 28% of the latter. The two other organizational contexts are intermediate in their accuracy—41% of those directed and analyzed by newspaper or station staff and 39% of those handled by a combination of staff and outside consultant are in the high-accuracy tercile.

The low likelihood of accuracy in polls conducted by professional researchers on the sponsoring station or newspaper staff is surprising and may be due to the assignment of poll responsibilities to marketing research professionals with little or no experience in polling. In this context, it is relevant to note that 41% of the polls conducted by national polling organizations (including the major network-newspaper polls) are in the high-accuracy tercile, compared with 32% of those conducted by nonnational organizations (see Table 8.5). While this is not a statistically significant difference, the patterning of accuracy suggests that polls handled by in-house staff researchers of media that do not maintain a separate polling department (as do the networks, the *New York Times*, the *Washington Post*, and the *Los Angeles Times*) are the

TABLE 8.4 / ACCURACY AND WHO DESIGNS AND ANALYZES POLLS

Accuracy Tercile	Media Staff (%)	Professional on Staff (%)	Outside Consultant (%)	Staff Researcher and Outside Consultant (%)	Outside Research Firm (%)
High	41	28	33	39	47
Medium	34	39	22	35	29
Low	25	33	45	26	24
Total	100	100	100	100	100
Number of polls	(32)	(142)	(9)	(57)	(79)

most susceptible to large error. It also suggests that the relatively high accuracy of polls conducted by the media staff noted above is accounted for by the national media's having separate polling departments.

Interviewing Staffs

The two most common types of interviewing staffs that were used for the polls in the quantitative survey are (1) paid interviewers who are hired and supervised by a member of the sponsoring paper's or station's staff (49%), and (2) interviewers of outside full-service survey research firms (36%) (see Table 8.6). Interviewing services were used for 12% of the polls, while 3% were conducted by organizations that made other arrangements, such as employing college students.

The nature of the interviewing staff is significantly related to poll accuracy. Of the polls that used interviewers from full-service research firms, 48% are in the high-accuracy tercile (see Table 8.7). This compares with 37% of the polls that used an outside interviewing service and 25% of the polls that used paid interviewers who were trained and supervised by a member of the paper's or station's staff. With respect to the last category, it is again necessary to note that although the major network-newspaper polls train and supervise their own interviewing staffs, these tasks are managed by separate polling departments that function like independent survey organizations. Also, they use central location telephone facilities, which, as noted below, are associated with rela-

TABLE 8.5 / ACCURACY AND THE SCOPE OF POLLING ORGANIZATIONS

Accuracy Tercile	National Polls (%)	State or Local Polls (%)
High	41	32
Medium	30	34
Low	30	34
Total	101*	100
Number of polls	(64)	(356)

*Total is more than 100% because of rounding.

TABLE 8.6 / TYPE OF INTERVIEWING STAFF

		Accuracy Tercile		
Interviewing Staff	All Polls (%)	High (%)	Medium (%)	Low (%)
Outside full-service survey research firm	36	50	28	29
Outside interviewing service	12	12	9	14
Paid interviewers trained and supervised by a member of the paper's or station's staff	49	35	59	53
College students, as class assignment	1	1	2	—
Other	2	2	2	4
Total	100	100	100	100
Number of polls	(366)	(123)	(124)	(110)

tively high accuracy. This suggests that it is specifically the local media, which extemporize and do not have the permanent resources of the networks, that are characterized by large errors.

Interviewing Facilities

Over three-fourths (77%) of all the polls in the quantitative survey were conducted by organizations that utilize central location facilities, compared with 12% that were conducted by telephone from the interviewers' homes (see Table 8.8). Since a central location facility was used for most of the polls, it is not surprising that only 28% of the polls conducted in this manner are in the high-accuracy tercile. Even so, a still smaller proportion—12%—of the seventeen polls conducted from interviewers' homes are in the high-accuracy tercile (see Table 8.9). The very low accuracy associated with the latter procedure undoubtedly reflects inferior training and supervision. Additionally, it seems likely that the use of this method reflects a willingness to cut corners that affects other methodological and design characteristics, and quality controls, as well.

TABLE 8.7 / ACCURACY AND TYPE OF INTERVIEWING STAFF

Accuracy Tercile	Outside Full-Service Firm (%)	Outside Interviewing Service (%)	Interviewers Trained and Supervised by Media Staff (%)
High	48	37	25
Medium	27	27	42
Low	25	37	33
Total	100	101*	100
Number of polls	(128)	(41)	(174)

*Total is more than 100% because of rounding.

TABLE 8.8 / TYPE OF INTERVIEWING FACILITY

Interviewing Facility	All Polls (%)	Accuracy Tercile		
		High (%)	Medium (%)	Low (%)
Central location telephone	77	75	75	83
Telephone from interviewer's home	12	4	16	11
More than one facility	6	7	5	6
Other	5	13	4	—
Total	100	99*	100	100
Number of polls	(155)	(44)	(55)	(52)

*Total is less than 100% because of rounding.

TABLE 8.9 / ACCURACY AND TELEPHONE INTERVIEWING FACILITY

Accuracy Tercile	Location of Interviewer	
	Central Facility (%)	At Home (%)
High	28	12
Medium	35	53
Low	37	35
Total	100	100
Number of polls	(117)	(17)

ATTENTION TO METHODOLOGY

Of the polls in the quantitative survey, 36% were conducted by organizations that noted they had "recently" changed their poll methodology (see Table 8.10). Of those polls, 44% are in the high-accuracy tercile, compared with 30% of the polls conducted by organizations that have not changed their poll methodology (see Table 8.11). This difference is statistically significant. It seems reasonable to infer that changing one's methodology indicates that one has been conducting pre-election polls over a period of time and/or that resources have been committed to improving poll performance. That is, polling accuracy is associated with experience in polling and efforts to improve methods.

TABLE 8.10 / RECENT CHANGES IN POLL METHODOLOGY

| | | Accuracy Tercile | | |
Changes in Methodology	All Polls (%)	High (%)	Medium (%)	Low (%)
Recent changes made	36	46	32	30
Recent changes not made	64	54	68	70
Total	100	100	100	100
Number of polls	(336)	(114)	(115)	(98)

TABLE 8.11 / ACCURACY AND RECENT CHANGES IN METHODOLOGY

Accuracy Tercile	Recent Changes Made (%)	Recent Changes Not Made (%)
High	44	30
Medium	31	37
Low	25	33
Total	100	100
Number of polls	(118)	(209)

SUMMARY

The above relationships between organization characteristics and accuracy are not conclusive, but they do suggest that willingness to make a major commitment of resources is an important correlate of poll accuracy. Once account is taken of the commitment of major resources by the national network-newspaper polls, an important correlate of error appears to be an *ad hoc* use by media of their in-house research facilities and capabilities originally intended for other purposes.

9 / A Multivariate Analysis

We have seen that the accuracy of pre-election polls is related to a number of methodological and contextual characteristics. Moreover, some of these characteristics are themselves correlated with each other. The question arises, therefore, as to how the combination of associated characteristics acts together to affect accuracy. This question has been answered in part by testing for the significance of differences between pairs of means for cells created by multivariate cross-tabulations. To further answer this question, a regression analysis was performed using data from the quantitative survey, with the accuracy of pre-election polls the dependent variable. The specific purpose of this regression analysis was to ascertain the percentage of the variance in accuracy that is explained by a number of specified characteristics measured in the quantitative survey.

As described in Chapter 2, the data from the methodological questionnaire were subject to problems of colinearity stemming from the linking of information from each polling organization to all the pre-election polls it had conducted. For this reason, most of the variables from the methodological questionnaire could not be

included in the regression analysis. Instead, only those variables that provide a unique value for each poll were used.

As an indicator of any underlying "house effect" common to polls conducted by any one organization, one variable from the methodology questionnaire—the importance of poll accuracy—was included in the regression analysis as an independent variable. There are two reasons for selecting this characteristic. First, it has a significant relation to accuracy, as measured by the relation between importance and the proportion of polls in the high-accuracy tercile. Second, it relates to a general characteristic of an organization that apparently influences all of its methodology. This variable allows us at least partially to account for the influence of the house effect on polling accuracy without including a number of highly colinear organization variables.

Seven other variables were also used as independent variables. Four of them relate to the political context of the election—whether it was a primary or general election, whether an incumbent was running, the extent of voter turnout, and the margin of victory. The other three—the size of the sample, the percentage of undecided voters, and the timing of interviewing in relation to the day of election—are aspects of methodology that are unique to each poll.

In five instances, actual values were used; in the other three, dummy variables were used. The eight independent variables (x_1–x_8) and their scoring are as follows:

x_1 Whether the poll was for a primary election: 1,0

x_2 Whether an incumbent was running for reelection: 1,0

x_3 The size of the sample used in the poll: actual number

x_4 The number of days before the election during which the poll was completed: actual number

x_5 The proportion of all voting-age adults in the jurisdiction covered by the poll that voted in the election: actual percentage

x_6 The margin of victory of the winning candidate over the second-place candidate: in percentage points

x_7 The percentage undecided in the poll: actual percentage

x_8 Whether accuracy is rated very important, fairly important, not too important, or not at all important: 1,2,3,4

The dependent variable, y, is the difference in percentage points between the percentage of the total vote received by the winning

candidate and his or her percentage in the poll after allocating the undecided vote.

A step-wise regression was performed so that the improvement in explained variance as each successive variable is introduced to the model can be evaluated. The results of the analysis appear in Table 9.1. The zero order correlation of each independent variable with accuracy is also shown.

It is noteworthy that, as discussed earlier, sample size does not enter into the regression model at all despite the significant zero order correlation between it and accuracy. That is, while sample size is correlated with accuracy, as would be expected, once the other variables are considered, differences in sample size do not improve our ability to explain why some polls are more accurate than others. The failure of sample size to add to explained variance is particularly striking in light of the small proportion of variance, .124, explained by the total model. (That the model does not explain a larger proportion of the variance is undoubtedly due to the fact that it does not include a number of methodological variables that, as we have seen, are related to accuracy.)

The small gains in explained variance after the second step are also noteworthy. In this connection, it should be noted that the margin of victory, which enters the model in step 2, subsequently is the last variable to enter the model at every step but the seventh, when importance of accuracy enters last. It should also be noted that turnout and primary elections are highly correlated, with a zero order correlation of $-.74$.

Because of the high correlation between turnout and primary elections, two additional regressions were conducted, using the same independent variables but with turnout excluded in one model and primary elections excluded in the other. In both instances, sample size was retained as an independent variable. In order to evaluate the contribution of each variable to explained variance in these analyses, beta values were calculated for each in addition to B values. (A principle components analysis was conducted to test whether after removing primary elections and turnout respectively from each model there was any remaining problem of colinearity. Colinearity would be a problem if two or more variables have high loadings on a component that accounts for a small proportion of total variance. No such instances were found.)

The results of these two regressions are shown in Table 9.2. The

TABLE 9.1 / BETA VALUES FOR INDEPENDENT VARIABLES

Variable	r	Step 1	Step 2	Step 3	Step 4	Step 5	Step 6	Step 7
Intercept		4.32	3.56	4.96	4.33	4.31	4.70	3.90
Number of days to election	.21	0.12	0.11	0.11	0.10	0.10	0.10	0.10
Margin of victory	.16	—	0.06	0.05	0.05	0.05	0.04	0.04
Turnout	-.19	—	—	-3.28	-2.73	-3.46	-3.69	-2.21
Percentage undecided	.17	—	—	—	0.03	0.03	0.03	0.03
Incumbent in race	.00	—	—	—	—	0.65	0.70	0.69
Importance of accuracy	-.11	—	—	—	—	—	-0.63	-0.66
Primary election	.16	—	—	—	—	—	—	0.85
Sample size	-.15	—	—	—	—	—	—	—
R^2		.059	.095	.110	.115	.119	.122	.124
F		21.6	17.9	14.1	11.0	9.1	7.8	6.9
$p > F$		.0001	.0001	.0001	.0001	.0001	.0001	.0001

TABLE 9.2 / COMPARISON OF TWO REGRESSION MODELS

Variable	Excluding Primary		Excluding Turnout	
	Parameter Values	Beta Values	Parameter Values	Beta Values
Intercept	4.87		3.08	
Number of days to election	0.096	0.21	0.095	0.20
Margin of victory	0.040	0.14	0.050	0.15
Turnout	−3.450	−0.13	x	x
Primary election	x	x	1.360	0.12
Percentage unde-cided	0.030	0.07	0.030	0.08
Incumbent in race	0.700	0.07	0.540	0.06
Importance of accu-racy	−0.550	−0.05	−0.540	−0.05
Sample size	0.000	−0.04	0.000	−0.04
R^2	.12		.12	
F	6.75		6.74	
p > F	.0001		.0001	

x = not included in regression equation.

two models show almost identical results, which is to be expected given the high correlation between primary elections and turnout. Examining the beta values, we see that after controlling for the influence of the other variables, the closeness of a pre-election poll to the election has the largest association with accuracy. Ranking next are margin of victory and either turnout or whether the election is a primary. The remaining variables—the percentage unde-cided, whether there is an incumbent in the race, the importance of accuracy to the polling organization, and sample size—contribute little more to the explanatory power of the model. This analysis clarifies some of the relationships to poll accuracy previously identified.

The fact that a poll's timing has the largest beta values indicates that missing last-minute changes in voting preference is one of the more significant sources of polling error, in general as well as in primary elections. This underscores the need to think of voting intentions as labile rather than fixed psychological states. Only as voting preferences crystallize, and only to the extent that they do,

can pre-election polls be reliable indicators of election outcome. In one sense, this conclusion supports the position of pollsters who argue against treating pre-election polls as predictions. On the other hand, the fact that accuracy is improved by conducting polls close to an election indicates that it is meaningful to compare the accuracy of pre-election polls on the same election that were conducted close to that election (and equally close) and to use accuracy as a criterion for evaluating the quality of polls conducted immediately before an election.

Two likely explanations for the relatively large beta values for the margin of victory in both models relate to issues that arose during the personal interviews. In those interviews, some pollsters observed that in landslide elections (1) a proportion of the victor's supporters do not bother to vote, and (2) a proportion of the victor's supporters who are potential defectors from their party of preference "return to the fold." It also appears likely that voting preference and/or intention to vote is held more strongly in closely contested elections than in those with sizable margins of victory, adding another dimension to attitudinal lability. The possibility that margins of victory are consistently overstated in polls on elections with incumbents can be ruled out in light of the small zero order correlation ($r = .03$) between incumbency and margin of victory.

The virtual interchangeability of turnout and whether an election is a primary, coupled with the relatively large beta values of each factor, reflects the difficulty pollsters have experienced in developing a satisfactory method for identifying likely voters in low-turnout elections. Since closeness of the poll to the election is controlled in these models, it also seems that the combination of low turnout and difficulty in conducting pre-primary polls very close to an election accounts for the sizable errors associated with many of these polls.

In interpreting the very small beta values for sample size, account needs to be taken of its correlation with turnout (.28) and whether an election is a primary ($-.27$). That is, small samples tend to be used for polls on low-turnout elections and primaries. Once the association between accuracy and those types of elections is controlled, increasing the sample size does not add to accuracy. Apparently, very large samples are not needed for accu-

racy, undoubtedly because increasing the sample size does not correct for nonrandom measurement error even though it does narrow confidence bands. An efficient use of resources for increasing accuracy, once minimum sample size requirements are met, would be to apply them to the development of better methods for identifying likely voters in low-turnout elections and to the development of procedures for monitoring trends in voter preference in the final days of a campaign.

10 / Conclusions

The Social Science Research Council's investigation of the performance of pre-election polls in the 1948 presidential election identified four major sources or error: (1) the use of flawed sample designs, (2) failure to screen nonvoters out of the sample, (3) inadequate methods for treating "undecided" responses, and (4) failure to measure late changes in voting preference. This study has examined these and other aspects of the research designs now used in pre-election polls. It has also examined additional issues related to the political context of election campaigns as well as to selected characteristics of polling organizations.

It is apparent that to an appreciable degree, the sources of error in pre-election polls that were identified in the SSRC's study are still present and continue to be important. Many pre-election polls are still characterized by relatively crude, *ad hoc* research designs that make no more than partial use of state-of-the-art methodology. To varying degrees, this crudity can be ascribed to the inexperience and, in some instances, lack of professional training of newcomers who have been attracted to polling by the proliferation of media-sponsored polls. It must also be recognized that inadequate budgets are undoubtedly a problem for many with the req-

uisite skill and experience. But other influences have also been at work.

In evaluating those other sources of inaccuracy in pre-election polling, it should be recognized that some organizations have developed and/or adopted methods that, to a considerable degree, correct the methodological inadequacies identified in the 1948 polls, most notably with respect to sample designs. Even in those instances, however, pre-election polls have been subject to considerable error that cannot be explained by sampling error. That is, all pre-election polls, including those that adhere to sampling theory, are subject to appreciable nonsampling error. It seems likely that the stress placed on sampling error in media reports, usually to the exclusion of nonsampling error, can lead to unrealistic expectations of the accuracy of pre-election polls. Since simply through chance a fair proportion of pre-election polls may "correctly" point to the winner, when large errors do occur, they are apt to be seen as unusual failures to be explained by the special characteristics of a particular election. By diverting attention from the magnitude of nonrandom error that is typical of pre-election polls, an exclusive stress on sampling error can have the unanticipated effect of deemphasizing the need for correcting the sources of nonsampling error.

RELIANCE ON PERSONAL JUDGMENT

It has not always been apparent how to apply theoretical principles to the sometimes conflicting practical problems encountered in pre-election polling. Often, extensive and costly methodological research is necessary before theoretically sound means of dealing with those problems can be developed. In too few cases have the time or funds been allocated for such research. Furthermore, few pollsters have published the results of whatever in-house methodological studies they may have conducted. The resultant paucity of the methodological literature on pre-election polling has forced most practitioners to rely primarily on their often limited in-house resources. Also, as noted above, large polling errors are often "explained" by reference to the unique qualities of a particular election rather than by reference to inadequacies in re-

search designs. Exacerbating this situation is the belief, expressed by many pollsters who fail to distinguish between scientific methodology and the skill with which it is applied, that polling is as much "art" as science. The consequence of all this is that many pollsters have relied upon personal judgment rather than methodological research to deal with the more intractable problems with which they have had to cope.

While judgment is always subject to personal bias, it should not surprise us if there is concurrence in the judgment of highly experienced and well-trained pollsters. When such consensus exists, we have tentatively assumed a face validity. However, we have also seen that pollsters often disagree as to the best solution for some problems—even when they agree on the importance and nature of the problem. Those conflicts in judgment illustrate the risk in accepting without further research the recommendations of even the most experienced researchers.

Even when a consensus of judgment exists, its validity should be verified by systematic testing. In some (but not all) cases, the findings of the quantitative survey have performed this function. These findings have helped resolve some of the disagreements among pollsters. Where they have not, the opposing points of view have been used to specify alternative hypotheses for further methodological research.

ACCURACY AS A GOAL OF PRE-ELECTION POLLS

Many professional pollsters have reacted to the magnitude of nonsampling error in their pre-election polls by eschewing "accuracy" as a goal and substituting "analysis" as their objective. Furthermore, a surprising number of those interviewed in the qualitative phase of the study expressed limited confidence in their methodology for achieving anything more than a rough approximation of candidates' standing, stressing the "softness" of pre-election polls.

While in one sense rejecting accuracy as a goal is "realistic," it can be self-defeating if it results in relying upon judgment and *ad hoc* improvisation to cope with nonrandom error rather than devoting resources to the development of more effective designs for

pre-election polls. Similarly, inferior sample designs can hardly be justified on the grounds that the goal is analysis rather than accuracy. Most important, the validity of any analysis based on imprecise measurements must be suspect. If pre-election polls are to have value for analyzing voting behavior and not only for journalism, methods for reducing both sampling and nonsampling error are essential.

Since pollsters who explicitly reject accuracy as their goal tend to avoid conducting their final pre-election polls in the closing days of a campaign, they are apt to miss any last-minute changes in voter preference. Thus, the analyses that they perform cannot automatically be extrapolated to actual election outcome. Furthermore, their analyses are geared primarily toward journalistic interpretations of election campaigns. While that is a valid objective for media-sponsored polls, it can reduce the pressure to produce more than an approximate assessment of voter preference. That is, the pressure to produce a highly accurate measurement at the time the poll is taken, as distinct from the pressure to produce accuracy in relation to the election itself, is eased. This may in part explain the willingness of some pollsters to employ methods that they recognize as "soft." To that extent, setting analysis as one's goal may be self-defeating.

SAMPLING

A major source of error in any survey is the use of a nonprobability sample design. It is, therefore, noteworthy that pre-election polls based on quota samples are not less accurate than those that do not use quotas and that those that interview any available adult are not less accurate than those that use a random respondent selection procedure. Before concluding that nonprobability samples are as good as probability samples in pre-election polls, these findings must be placed in perspective.

First, a valid comparison of the accuracy of polls based on probability and nonprobability sample designs must take into account the contributions of all design features to polling error and not only whether sample units are selected by probability methods. The results of this study suggest that the failure of polls based on probability designs to be more accurate than polls based on non-

probability designs is in all likelihood in part the result of such nonsample design characteristics as the closeness of interviewing to election day and the ability to identify likely voters. An evaluation of the effects of these two characteristics on polling design must consider the following two points:

1. Since on the average the most accurate polls are those that are conducted within days of an election, the interviewing schedule is a design feature that can have a major effect on the accuracy of polls based on probability samples. Probability sampling requires a full schedule of call-backs, so that a longer interviewing period is needed than when a nonprobability design is used. This makes it easier to conduct polls based on the latter design close to election day. As a result, polls based on probability samples are more likely to miss last-minute shifts in voting preferences than are polls based on nonprobability samples.

2. Accurate exclusion of nonvoters from the measurement base is another nonsampling design feature that needs to be taken into account in assessing probability versus nonprobability samples. Some pollsters who report they use probability designs also express dissatisfaction with their methods for differentiating between likely and unlikely voters. Their polls are susceptible to sizable error despite their sound sample designs, which would explain why they do not achieve a higher level of accuracy than do some users of nonprobability sample designs.

A second consideration is that the distinction between probability and nonprobability samples is blurred by the practices of many pollsters who use probability methods at most but not all stages of selection—so-called modified probability samples. Many, though by no means all, pollsters who utilize nonprobability methods nonetheless recognize the weaknesses of those methods and have modified their sample designs to control the most obvious sources of sample bias that are inherent in nonprobability samples. It appears that their use of quotas in the final stage of respondent selection in a poll that has used probability methods at all previous stages does not result in as severe a bias as would be expected if judgment and quota had been used at all stages.

The widely used nonprobability respondent selection procedure of youngest man/youngest, or oldest, woman is illustrative. This technique involves a sex quota and, in fact, accounts for the largest proportion of polls that use quotas. However, it does not rely on interviewer judgment and convenience, which are impor-

tant sources of bias in quota sampling. It does not eliminate bias, but when employed at the last stage of a poll in which all previous stages had used probability procedures, it apparently results in improved samples as compared with traditional quota samples—with a concomitant improvement in accuracy.

Some of the appeal of this technique to pollsters who otherwise utilize probability sampling derives from the need in pre-election polling to complete interviewing within the shortest feasible period of time. This limits the practicality of the theoretically superior procedure of randomly selecting respondents from all voting-age adults who reside in households drawn into the sample and then making repeated call-backs to complete the sample. On the other hand, in order to meet the time constraints to which they are subject, some pollsters who use probability methods fail to adhere to a full call-back schedule, with inevitable reductions in completion rates. The likely result is that their polls are subject to sample biases that reduce the initial superiority of their sample designs compared with designs that utilize sex quotas in conjunction with the youngest man/youngest woman technique.

Another factor that blurs the advantages of probability sampling is the use of sample weighting. We have seen that weighting corrects for much of the bias to which samples that use a combination of probability and quota are subject. Rather than indicating that the use of quotas in polls is acceptable, this finding emphasizes the contribution that the application of sampling theory makes to poll accuracy.

A third consideration is that some judgment samples are designed to control for voting participation, a political variable that is significantly related to accuracy but is often difficult to control when probability samples are used. It seems likely that the accuracy of pre-election polls based on probability samples would be improved if sample designs controlling for voting participation—either through stratification or weighting—were employed. Although some pollsters question its reliability, stratifying samples by turnout in previous comparable elections has been shown to contribute to accuracy. The use of such a variable as a weighting factor may be a practical alternative to stratification in telephone samples, where it is impossible to stratify the frame along appropriate political boundaries.

The contribution to accuracy that can be made by weighting for other political variables, such as political party identification, is questionable. Since trends in party identification tend to parallel shifts in voting preference for major offices, weighting by this factor is contraindicated for high-visibility elections. However, it might be a useful weighting factor in polls on elections for low-visibility offices, since party identification often is a major determinant of voting behavior in such elections.

Demographic weighting also contributes to accuracy, although there is some difference of opinion regarding which variables should be used. While the use of sex and, to a lesser degree, race or ethnicity and education as weighting variables is putative evidence of their utility, the specific contribution to accuracy that is made by weighting by each of these variables needs to be explicated. Furthermore, interaction effects between weighting variables must be specified in order that weighting by one factor not introduce new biases into the sample. That is, weighting models that can be used as standard elements of estimating procedure need to be applied. *Ad hoc* weighting when a sample appears to be biased on certain demographic characteristics can improve the "cosmetics" of a poll without necessarily improving accuracy. *Ad hoc* weighting and tested models are performed by pollsters who employ nonprobability samples and by those who use probability sampling. Thus, some pre-election polls that are based on samples that incorporate nonprobability design elements may in some respects be methodologically superior to some that do not use nonprobability methods.

The use of telephone samples is also pertinent to any evaluation of sampling designs employed in pre-election polls. Despite the near universality of telephone households nationally, and despite the use of random digit dialing to ensure the inclusion of unlisted numbers within the sample frame, the underrepresentation of racial and ethnic minorities even in probability telephone samples can be appreciable. The effect of such a bias may be limited in national polls but is reported to be sizable in states and local communities with large minority populations. Weighting by race or ethnicity does not correct for the exclusion of nontelephone households or for the likely bias when the completion rate among minority telephone households is particularly low. Thus, polls

that use probability samples may be as biased, and perhaps even more biased, with respect to minority representation, as are those that resort to quotas to ensure the proportionate representation of minorities.

Finally, large noncompletion rates appear to be a particular problem in pre-election polls based on telephone probability samples. Although telephone interviewing has provided pollsters with better access to most households than does personal interviewing, this advantage has apparently been neutralized by high refusal rates. The refusal problem has been intensified by the common practice of making a limited number of call-backs. As previously noted, this practice is related to the time constraints typical of pre-election polls. Additionally, some pollsters justify it by claiming that call-backs are not productive since nonvoters are disproportionately represented in the call-back interviews. Regardless of the merits of this justification, the distinction in quality between polls based on probability designs that nonetheless accept high noncompletion rates and those that use nonprobability methods only at the final stage of respondent selection is more apparent than real.

In summary, the comparable accuracy of pre-election polls based on samples that do and do not incorporate nonprobability design features appears to be the product of two countervailing influences:

1. Probability sampling as used by some pollsters is nonetheless deficient in important design features. The result is that pre-election polls based on such samples are susceptible to significant bias.

2. Some pollsters who use samples that include nonprobability design elements have empirically developed procedures that compensate to varying degrees for the theoretical inadequacies of their samples. Moreover, by concentrating their resources on problems such as timing and turnout, they have controlled sources of polling error that cannot be solved merely by using probability samples.

Rote applications of probability sampling by themselves will not produce accurate pre-election polls. While it should not come as a surprise that good research requires more than superficial conformity to probability sampling, the prevalence of nonprobability

samples in pre-election polling has led some to overlook the practical problems that must be solved before theoretically acceptable sample designs can be satisfactorily used in pre-election polls. Further controversy regarding the merits of probability and non-probability samples is sterile. Instead, attention needs to be directed to asking how probability sampling can be successfully employed in pre-election polling.

TURNOUT

Many pollsters use admittedly inadequate methods for measuring registration status and identifying likely voters. They do this even though experience in many, though not all, elections is that candidates' standing can be significantly changed by using alternative methods for identifying likely voters. Thus, polls that would otherwise be within the sampling error of election results may nonetheless be in considerable error because an invalid method was used to identify likely voters. Furthermore, the consensus is that one of the weakest design features of most polls is their inability to correctly identify likely voters, especially in low-turnout elections. Thus, the scientific study of low-turnout elections, such as primaries, off-year elections, and local elections, is limited by the lack of improvement in methods for identifying likely voters.

With a few exceptions, the common practice is to use crude methods and rely on judgment to compensate for the lack of a better method. The exceptions, in contrast, indicate that setting as a goal the improved accuracy in identifying likely voters and devoting the resources to achieve it have resulted in improved methods for identifying likely voters. These exceptions indicate some promising approaches to this problem.

With respect to registration status, inflated self-reports have been reduced by (1) including a socially acceptable negative response alternative in the question wording, (2) specifying whether the respondent is currently registered to vote from his or her current address, and, (3) as appropriate, determining whether the respondent's registration has been updated. Simply asking whether one is registered is not sufficient.

It is also clear that differentiating with precision between likely

and nonlikely voters among the registered requires a battery of items rather than one or two screening questions. Such a battery should include measures of intent, knowledge about the electoral process, intensity of feelings and motivation, and political involvement in the specific election. The application of scaling models to such a battery rather than employing *ad hoc* scoring schemes is also indicated. Further analysis of scale items to identify objectively a "cutting point" or to develop a model to assign a probability of voting weight to each respondent, rather than using judgment to estimate turnout rate, is another promising avenue for methodological development.

MEASURING CANDIDATE PREFERENCE

Methodological research is needed as well in regard to the question that asks for candidate preference. The near consensus is that the best method is not to ask for the respondent's future voting intention but, rather, to ask for preference in a manner that simulates the voting booth as closely as is feasible. Those few pollsters who have used a "secret" paper ballot in personal interviews testify to the efficacy of that method. Simulating the voting booth in a telephone interview is more problematic. Although most polls take a similar approach in asking for preference, variations in the details of question wording may exert measurable, but at this time unknown, effects on expressed preference.

Measuring preference for low-visibility offices presents special problems. There is a considerable body of opinion among pollsters that expressions of preference for such offices may not adequately reflect the relative influence of familiarity with the candidates' names, coattail effects, and party loyalty. Until question wordings that cope with these problems are developed, the utility of pre-election polls for the study of voting behavior in local elections will be limited. Methodological issues that need to be resolved include the effect of presenting complete tickets versus measuring preference for individual races, order of presentation of candidates' names and offices at stake, the ability of respondents to handle lengthy lists in telephone interviews, and the use of identifiers of the candidates' background.

Pre-election polls have achieved considerable success in measuring preference as a discrete psychological state measurable by a single item, even though voting intentions are affected by the interaction of established habit, group identifications, beliefs, values, and feelings. Despite the analytic value in measuring these influences, it is apparently not necessary to do so for a pre-election poll to be accurate. Efforts to measure voting preference by modeling these influences must make assumptions as to their relative weight and how they interact with each other, assumptions that usually have no basis other than in judgment. In contrast, if preference is validly measured by direct questioning, it can be used as an independent variable to test alternative causal models. This is another reason why more attention needs to be paid to testing the validity of alternative question wordings. One technique that warrants further investigation in comparison with the typical format is the constant sum technique.

Pre-election polls with a large undecided vote are more prone to error than are those with a small undecided vote. Since the size of the undecided vote is in part an artifact of the measurement methods used, this relationship must be interpreted cautiously. Nonetheless, when the undecided vote is minimized, error is reduced. In part, reducing the undecided vote involves eliminating nonvoters from the measurement base, an indication that many undecided respondents do not have a preference. Other undecided respondents do have preferences, but those preferences are either weak or else the respondents are reluctant to voice them. Leaner questions are an effective, and widely used, probe to measure the preferences of this segment of the undecided vote. But the contribution of leaner probes to accuracy is contingent upon first screening out likely nonvoters. If that is not done, there is a danger that measured preference will be contaminated by nonattitudes.

Determining the "true" size of the undecided vote requires, at a minimum, differentiating between those who have no preference because they are uninvolved in the election and those who are involved but have not been able to make up their mind. While standard question wordings do not attempt to make such a differentiation, a cross-analysis by likelihood of voting appears to be an

effective way of isolating the uninvolved. How best to allocate the undecided likely voters after a leaner probe remains problematic.

INTERVIEWING DATES AND THE LABILITY OF VOTING PREFERENCE

As pollsters have long maintained, the accuracy of pre-election polls as indicators of election outcome is very much dependent on scheduling the polls as closely as possible to the date of the election. This is reassuring to the extent that it indicates that measured preferences can correlate with voting behavior. On the other hand, it also emphasizes the susceptibility of candidate preference to change, a susceptibility that raises questions as to the meaning of pre-election polls, especially those conducted more than a few days before election day. Predicting elections on the basis of pre-election polls is based on the assumption that preferences will not change in the interim between interviewing and voting. And, as to be expected, the shorter the interim, the greater is the likelihood of that assumption's holding true. Thus, the predictive power of pre-election polls is contingent not only upon how accurately they measure preference among the voting electorate at the time of interviewing, but also on the likelihood that those preferences will not change. It follows that analytic studies of the electoral process would be enhanced if their designs incorporated valid measures of change and propensity to change.

Elections differ in their chronologies, in particular, the point of a campaign at which preferences crystallize. In early-crystallizing elections, early pre-election polls may provide surprisingly good indications of the likely election outcome. When preferences crystallize late, however, early polls are subject to considerable error. In late-crystallizing elections, only late polls can be expected to provide an accurate basis for estimating the actual vote. The indications are that primaries and general elections for local and state offices are the most likely to be late crystallizing, so that early polls on such elections are especially prone to error. However, general elections for major offices, including the presidency, may under certain conditions crystallize late. For these reasons, determining whether preferences have crystallized, and when, is essential to the use of pre-election polls for predicting election outcome.

A number of assumptions as to what conditions determine when crystallization takes place are common among pollsters. These assumptions, which they have not tested, include whether one of the candidates is an incumbent, prior familiarity with the names of the candidates, how well structured are the beliefs held about each candidate, the visibility of the office at stake, and whether feelings toward the candidates are balanced or imbalanced. Also assumed to be of critical importance is the scheduling of campaign activities and the attention given to those activities by the news media. These assumptions define significant variables that should be considered when forming hypotheses as to the determinants of voter decision making in any election.

As the frequent irrelevance of early pre-election polls to ultimate voting behavior demonstrates, to understand voter decision making it is insufficient to analyze surveys taken even as close as ten to twelve days in advance of election day. Particularly with regard to late-crystallizing elections, a full understanding can be achieved only if earlier polls are analyzed in relation to last-minute surveys. To study the development of voter preference in an election, it is necessary to have accurate late indicators of voting preference as well as full profiles of voter cognitions, preferences, and values. A further consideration stems from the fact that an important aspect of crystallization is the decision as to whether one will vote. Therefore, to analyze the development of voter decision making, it is essential that after differentiating between likely and unlikely voters at successive stages of a campaign, one analyze the process of growing involvement in or dissociation from an election.

The susceptibility of candidate preference to change is also relevant to the more general issue of how verbal expressions of attitude relate to subsequent behavior. We have seen that it is only when the components of voter attitude have crystallized into a firm voting intention that high correlations between stated preferences and behavior can be expected. And even then, new experiences can lead to a restructuring of intentions, so that predictions of voting behavior based on earlier measurements will be subject to considerable error. That is, the predictive power of attitudinal measurements is contingent upon specifying the structure of at-

titudes at the time of measurement and the impact of subsequent situational influences upon that structure.

CONCLUSIONS

Pre-election polls as they are currently conducted are subject to sizable error, of a magnitude far greater than can be explained by sampling error alone. While some of the additional error can be ascribed to sample bias, much of it stems from nonsampling measurement error.

Although considerable improvement in sample designs used by pre-election polls has occurred, theoretically unsound methods are still common. Some of this divergence is probably due to a lack of appreciation and/or understanding of sampling theory and some to considerations of budget and convenience. In addition, there are operational considerations that inhibit the use of such procedures as random respondent selection and full call-back schedules. Telephone surveys present special sampling problems, in particular the achievement of satisfactory completion rates, forming appropriate frames for sampling on local and state elections, and the use of political variables in designing samples.

Problems in identifying likely voters remain a major potential source of nonsampling error, especially in low-turnout elections. Yet, a few pollsters who have devoted resources to developing satisfactory methods have achieved appreciable success. There is every reason to believe that even better methods can be developed if resources were made available.

Voting preferences are sometimes subject to large shifts within short time spans, so that only polls conducted immediately prior to an election can be expected to correspond consistently with election results. The development of validated methods for accurately measuring voting preference at any stage of a campaign can, therefore, be accomplished only by conducting pre-election polls in the final days of a campaign.

Question wordings designed to measure voting preference for high-visibility offices such as the presidency are less suitable for use in polls on low-visibility offices. Whether better methods can

be developed to simulate the act of voting when pre-election polls are conducted by telephone also needs to be investigated.

The lability of preference presents both a challenge and an opportunity for further research. On the one hand, instability of preference makes it difficult to assess when pre-election poll error is due to methodological failure and when it is due to change in preference. On the other hand, this instability is an important variable that needs to be analyzed if the process whereby voting decisions are reached is to be fully understood.

Two formidable barriers to improving poll accuracy go beyond the difficulties that are inherent in any program of methodological research. One is an apparent lack of awareness of, or commitment to, professional standards on the part of many, though not all, media sponsors. This is evident in the inadequate budgets they provide and in their acceptance of improvised, untested, and admittedly unsatisfactory methods and procedures. The other is an admitted preference of many pollsters and editors for judgmental interpretation over accurate measurement, a preference that results in criticisms regarding inaccuracy being written off as irrelevant to analytic journalism.

Until these barriers are overcome, it is likely that pre-election polls will, on the average, continue to be less accurate than need be the case. At this time, concern about surmounting such obstacles appears to be limited, so that the prospects for improvement in the near future must be rated as dim.

Questionnaire

Please have this questionnaire completed by the person
most familiar with the methods used to conduct your
pre-election polls—yourself, staff member, consultant,
or individual in an outside survey organization, as appropriate.

CONFIDENTIALITY: We guarantee that replies to this questionnaire will be kept confidential and will not in any way be identified with individual polls. The data will be analyzed statistically in a manner that will make it impossible for anyone to identify the particular methods of any polling organization. However, to maintain statistical control over the data, it is necessary for us to number the questionnaires.

PRIVILEGED INFORMATION: If you feel that a particular question asks you to divulge what you consider to be a trade secret, please skip that question—but, please do answer the other questions.

INSTRUCTIONS

Please describe the standard method *now* used to conduct your pre-election polls.

If your methods differ when conducting *final* pre-election polls as compared with earlier polls, please describe the *final pre-election poll methodology only*.

If any of your methods have changed in recent years, we would appreciate your describing these changes in the space provided on the last page.

Space is provided to describe methods used for pre-election polls related to National, State, and Local (city, county, Congressional District, etc.) general elections, and for primaries at all levels.

Please answer separately for each type of pre-election poll you conduct. *Cross out column for those types of polls you do NOT conduct.* Please check only one response per question in the remaining columns, except where otherwise noted.

RETURN TO: Dr. Irving Crespi
c/o Bureau of Social Science Research
1990 M Street, N.W.
Washington, D.C. 20036

A stamped return envelope is enclosed for your convenience.

	FINAL PRE-ELECTION POLL METHOD			
	General Elections			Primaries
	National	State	Local	
A. INTERVIEWING METHOD				
Personal in-home	1[ ]	1[ ]	1[ ]	1[ ]
Telephone: from central location	2[ ]	2[ ]	2[ ]	2[ ]
Telephone: from interviewer's home	3[ ]	3[ ]	3[ ]	3[ ]
Sidewalk, mall intercept	4[ ]	4[ ]	4[ ]	4[ ]
Phone-in	5[ ]	5[ ]	5[ ]	5[ ]
Mail	6[ ]	6[ ]	6[ ]	6[ ]
B. INTERVIEWING HOURS:				
Check as many as apply				
Weekday: daytime and evening	1[ ]	1[ ]	1[ ]	1[ ]
Weekday: daytime only	2[ ]	2[ ]	2[ ]	2[ ]
Weekday: evening only	3[ ]	3[ ]	3[ ]	3[ ]
Saturday	4[ ]	4[ ]	4[ ]	4[ ]
Sunday	5[ ]	5[ ]	5[ ]	5[ ]
C. ASSIGNED DEMOGRAPHIC QUOTAS:				
Check as many as are assigned				
None	1[ ]	1[ ]	1[ ]	1[ ]
Sex	2[ ]	2[ ]	2[ ]	2[ ]
Age	3[ ]	3[ ]	3[ ]	3[ ]
Race/ethnicity	4[ ]	4[ ]	4[ ]	4[ ]
Employed/not employed	5[ ]	5[ ]	5[ ]	5[ ]
Income	6[ ]	6[ ]	6[ ]	6[ ]
Education	7[ ]	7[ ]	7[ ]	7[ ]
Other: please describe _____ _____	8[ ]	8[ ]	8[ ]	8[ ]
D. POPULATION INTERVIEWED				
All voting age adults for entire questionnaire	1[ ]	1[ ]	1[ ]	1[ ]
Registered voters for entire questionnaire, plus non-registered for demographics only	2[ ]	2[ ]	2[ ]	2[ ]
Registered voters only. Screen out non-registered voters	3[ ]	3[ ]	3[ ]	3[ ]
Likely voters for entire questionnaire, plus unlikely voters for demographic questions	4[ ]	4[ ]	4[ ]	4[ ]
Likely voters only. Screen out unlikely voters	5[ ]	5[ ]	5[ ]	5[ ]
Other: please describe _____ _____	6[ ]	6[ ]	6[ ]	6[ ]

In Primaries, what do you do about cross-over voting? _____

	FINAL PRE-ELECTION POLL METHOD			
	General Elections			
	National	State	Local	Primaries
E. RESPONDENT SELECTED TO BE INTERVIEWED				
Available voting age adult	1[ ]	1[ ]	1[ ]	1[ ]
Youngest man/youngest woman at home	2[ ]	2[ ]	2[ ]	2[ ]
"Next birthday" selection procedure	3[ ]	3[ ]	3[ ]	3[ ]
Random selection from listing of household members	4[ ]	4[ ]	4[ ]	4[ ]
Other: please describe _____				
	5[ ]	5[ ]	5[ ]	5[ ]
F. NOT-AT-HOME				
If no one is at home, or the selected respondent is not at home, do you:				
Substitute	1[ ]	1[ ]	1[ ]	1[ ]
Weight by times-at-home	2[ ]	2[ ]	2[ ]	2[ ]
Conduct call-backs	3[ ]	3[ ]	3[ ]	3[ ]
None of above	4[ ]	4[ ]	4[ ]	4[ ]
G. REFUSALS				
When a respondent refuses to be interviewed, is another attempt made at another time to obtain an interview with the same person?				
Yes, as standard procedure	1[ ]	1[ ]	1[ ]	1[ ]
Yes, for some elections	2[ ]	2[ ]	2[ ]	2[ ]
No	3[ ]	3[ ]	3[ ]	3[ ]
H. WEIGHTING/ADJUSTING THE SAMPLE				
1. Do you weight the sample?				
Yes, as standard procedure	1[ ]	1[ ]	1[ ]	1[ ]
Yes, if necessary	2[ ]	2[ ]	2[ ]	2[ ]
No	3[ ]	3[ ]	3[ ]	3[ ]
2. IF YES: What sample weights are used? (Check as many as apply)				
Sex	1[ ]	1[ ]	1[ ]	1[ ]
Age	2[ ]	2[ ]	2[ ]	2[ ]
Race/ethnicity	3[ ]	3[ ]	3[ ]	3[ ]
Education	4[ ]	4[ ]	4[ ]	4[ ]
Income	5[ ]	5[ ]	5[ ]	5[ ]
Political party identification	6[ ]	6[ ]	6[ ]	6[ ]
Size of household	7[ ]	7[ ]	7[ ]	7[ ]
Other: please describe _____				
	8[ ]	8[ ]	8[ ]	8[ ]
3. Do you use any ratio or regression procedures to adjust the sample for divergences from known characteristics?				
Yes: for what characteristics? _____	1[ ]	1[ ]	1[ ]	1[ ]
No	2[ ]	2[ ]	2[ ]	2[ ]

	FINAL PRE-ELECTION POLL METHOD			
	General Elections			
	National	State	Local	Primaries
I. THE UNDECIDED VOTE				
Do you seek to reduce or allocate the "Undecided" vote? (IF YES): How? (Check as many as apply)				
Follow-up "leaner" question	1[ ]	1[ ]	1[ ]	1[ ]
Use opinions on issues	2[ ]	2[ ]	2[ ]	2[ ]
Use ratings of candidates	3[ ]	3[ ]	3[ ]	3[ ]
Party identification of undecided	4[ ]	4[ ]	4[ ]	4[ ]
Other: please describe _____				
_____	5[ ]	5[ ]	5[ ]	5[ ]
No, do not reduce or allocate	6[ ]	6[ ]	6[ ]	6[ ]
J. TURNOUT				
1. Do you report candidate standings for: (Check all that you report):				
All voting-age adults	1[ ]	1[ ]	1[ ]	1[ ]
Registered voters	2[ ]	2[ ]	2[ ]	2[ ]
"Likely voters"	3[ ]	3[ ]	3[ ]	3[ ]
"High/moderate/low-turnout voters"	4[ ]	4[ ]	4[ ]	4[ ]
2. Which *one* of the following best describes how you identify "likely voters"?				
a. Ask one question about likelihood of voting in addition to registration and include as likely voters those who indicate they are certain to vote.	1[ ]	1[ ]	1[ ]	1[ ]
b. Ask a series of "screening" questions and include as likely voters only those who successfully pass all screens.	2[ ]	2[ ]	2[ ]	2[ ]
c. Develop a "turnout score" based on a series of questions related to likelihood of voting, and include as likely voters all those who score above a "cutting point."	3[ ]	3[ ]	3[ ]	3[ ]
d. Assign a probability of voting weight to each person in the sample using characteristics related to likelihood of voting	4[ ]	4[ ]	4[ ]	4[ ]
e. Other: Please describe _____				
_____	5[ ]	5[ ]	5[ ]	5[ ]
f. Do not identify "likely voters."	6[ ]	6[ ]	6[ ]	6[ ]

	FINAL PRE-ELECTION POLL METHOD			
	General Elections			Primaries
	National	State	Local	
3. What characteristics do you use to identify "likely voters"? (Check all that apply)				
Reported registration	1[ ]	1[ ]	1[ ]	1[ ]
Stated intention to vote	2[ ]	2[ ]	2[ ]	2[ ]
Commitment to candidate	3[ ]	3[ ]	3[ ]	3[ ]
Interest in election	4[ ]	4[ ]	4[ ]	4[ ]
Information on the election	5[ ]	5[ ]	5[ ]	5[ ]
Reported past voting	6[ ]	6[ ]	6[ ]	6[ ]
Demographic characteristics	7[ ]	7[ ]	7[ ]	7[ ]
Other: please describe _____ _____	8[ ]	8[ ]	8[ ]	8[ ]
Do not identify "likely voters"	9[ ]	9[ ]	9[ ]	9[ ]
4. Do you use past turnout rates to sample or to weight geographic areas, such as regions or sections of a state?				
Yes, to *sample* areas	1[ ]	1[ ]	1[ ]	1[ ]
Yes, to *weight* areas	2[ ]	2[ ]	2[ ]	2[ ]
Yes, *both* to sample and to weight	3[ ]	3[ ]	3[ ]	3[ ]
No, neither	4[ ]	4[ ]	4[ ]	4[ ]
K. HOUSEHOLD SELECTION: TELEPHONE INTERVIEWS How are telephone numbers selected?				
Sample registration list and get telephone numbers of those who are selected	1[ ]	1[ ]	1[ ]	1[ ]
Select sample of numbers to call from telephone directory	2[ ]	2[ ]	2[ ]	2[ ]
Select sample of numbers from telephone directory and generate numbers to call from them	3[ ]	3[ ]	3[ ]	3[ ]
Computer-generated random numbers	4[ ]	4[ ]	4[ ]	4[ ]
Other: please describe _____ _____	5[ ]	5[ ]	5[ ]	5[ ]
Don't conduct telephone interviews	6[ ]	6[ ]	6[ ]	6[ ]
L. HOUSEHOLD SELECTION: PERSONAL INTERVIEWS How are interviewing areas selected?				
From Census block statistics	1[ ]	1[ ]	1[ ]	1[ ]
"Starting addresses" from telephone directories	2[ ]	2[ ]	2[ ]	2[ ]
From registration lists	3[ ]	3[ ]	3[ ]	3[ ]
Other: please describe _____ _____	4[ ]	4[ ]	4[ ]	4[ ]
Don't conduct personal interviews	5[ ]	5[ ]	5[ ]	5[ ]

| | FINAL PRE-ELECTION POLL METHOD | | | |
| | General Elections | | | |
	National	State	Local	Primaries
M. OTHER SAMPLE DESIGN FEATURES				
1. What is the approximate sample size (after screening out unlikely voters) on which candidate standings are based?	___	___	___	___
Do not screen out unlikely voters	1[ ]	1[ ]	1[ ]	1[ ]
2. Do you use a clustered or unclustered sample design?				
Clustered	1[ ]	1[ ]	1[ ]	1[ ]
Unclustered	2[ ]	2[ ]	2[ ]	2[ ]
3. Do you use a stratified or unstratified sample design?				
Stratified	1[ ]	1[ ]	1[ ]	1[ ]
Unstratified	2[ ]	2[ ]	2[ ]	2[ ]
N. POSITION OF CANDIDATE PREFERENCE QUESTION				
Before attitude/issue questions	1[ ]	1[ ]	1[ ]	1[ ]
After attitude/issue questions	2[ ]	2[ ]	2[ ]	2[ ]
Do not ask attitude/issue questions	3[ ]	3[ ]	3[ ]	3[ ]
O. LENGTH OF INTERVIEW				
1. What is average length of interview, in minutes?	___	___	___	___
2. Are questions asked that are not related to the election?				
Yes	1[ ]	1[ ]	1[ ]	1[ ]
No	2[ ]	2[ ]	2[ ]	2[ ]

ORGANIZATIONAL STRUCTURE

1. Who *designs* and *analyzes* your pre-election polls?
   1[ ]   Newspaper or station staff.
   2[ ]   Professional researchers who are on paper's or station's staff.
   3[ ]   An outside consultant.
   4[ ]   Both staff researchers and consultant.
   5[ ]   An outside survey research firm.
   6[ ]   Other: please describe _____
   _____

2. What type of interviewing staff is used for your pre-election polls?
   1[ ] An outside *full-service* survey research firm.
   2[ ] An outside *interviewing service.*
   3[ ] Paid interviewers who are trained and supervised by a member of the paper's or station's staff.
   4[ ] Reporters or other regular staff personnel.
   5[ ] College students, as a class assignment.
   6[ ] Volunteers from civic and community organizations.
   7[ ] Other: please describe _____

3. Is a highly accurate prediction of elections an important criterion when evaluating the success of your pre-election polls?
   1[ ] An extremely important criterion
   2[ ] An important criterion
   3[ ] Not too important a criterion
   4[ ] Not at all important

PLEASE USE THIS SPACE TO DESCRIBE RECENT CHANGES
IN YOUR METHODS AND THE DATE OF CHANGE

THANK YOU VERY MUCH FOR YOUR ASSISTANCE

RETURN TO: Dr. Irving Crespi
c/o Bureau of Social Science Research
1990 M Street, N.W.
Washington, D.C. 20036

References

Adler, Kenneth. 1984. "Why the polls differed in the '84 election."
Paper presented at May 1985 Conference of the American Association for Public Opinion Research.

Bogart, Leo. 1972. *Silent Politics: Polls and the Awareness of Public Opinion.* New York: Wiley-Interscience.

Buchanan, William. 1986. "Election predictions: An empirical assessment." *Public Opinion Quarterly* 40:222–227.

Cantril, Albert H. 1980. *Polling on the Issues.* Cabin John, Md.: Seven
Locks Press.

Converse, Philip E., and Michael W. Traugott. 1987. "Assessing the
accuracy of polls and surveys." *Science* 234:1094–1098.

Crespi, Irving, and Dwight Morris. 1984. "Question order and the
measurement of candidate preference in the 1982 Connecticut elections." *Public Opinion Quarterly* 48:578–591.

Day, Richard. 1983. "The Illinois experience." Paper presented at
May 1983 Conference of the American Association for Public Opinion Research.

Fenwick, Ian, Frederick Wiseman, John F. Becker, and James R.
Heiman. 1982. "Classifying undecided voters in pre-election
polls." *Public Opinion Quarterly* 46:383–391.

Field, Mervin. 1981. "Presidential election polling: Are the states
righter?" *Public Opinion* 4:16–19,56.

Gallup Report. 1983. No. 3 (November).

————. 1986. No. 254 (November): inside back cover.

Gollin, Albert H. 1980. "Polls and the news media: A symposium."
Public Opinion Quarterly 44:4.

Hagan, Dan E., and Charlotte Meier Collier. 1983. "Must respondent
selection procedures for telephone surveys be invasive?" *Public
Opinion Quarterly* 47:547–556.

Hennessy, Bernard C., and Erna R. Hennessy. 1961. "The prediction
of close elections: comments on some 1960 polls." *Public Opinion
Quarterly* 25:405–411.

Katosh, John P., and Michael W. Traugott. 1981. "The consequences of validated and self-reported voting measures." *Public Opinion Quarterly* 45:419–535.

Kelley, Stanley, Jr. 1983. *Interpreting Elections*. Princeton, N.J.: Princeton University Press.

Kohut, Andrew. 1983. "Illinois politics confound the polls." *Public Opinion* 5:42.

Mendelsohn, Harold, and Irving Crespi. 1970. *Polls, Television, and the New Politics*. Scranton: Chandler.

Miller, Mungo. 1952. "The Waukegan study of voter turnout prediction." *Public Opinion Quarterly* 16:381–398.

Mosteller, Frederick, Herbert Hyman, Philip J. McCarthy, Eli S. Marks, and David B. Truman. 1948. The *Pre-election Polls of 1948*. New York: Social Science Research Council.

Perry, Paul. 1960. "Election survey procedures of the Gallup Poll." *Public Opinion Quarterly* 24:531–542.

———. 1962. "Gallup Poll election survey experience, 1950–1960." *Public Opinion Quarterly* 26:272–279.

———. 1965. "Election survey methods." *Gallup Political Index* 7:i–xii.

———. 1973. "A comparison of the voting preferences of likely and unlikely voters." *Public Opinion Quarterly* 37:99–109.

———. 1979. "Certain problems in election survey methodology." *Public Opinion Quarterly* 43:312–325.

Roll, Charles. 1968. "Straws in the wind: The record of The Daily News Poll." *Public Opinion Quarterly* 32:251–260.

Roll, Charles, and Albert H. Cantril. 1972. *Polls: Their Use and Misuse*. New York and London: Basic Books.

Roper, Burns. 1983. "Election poll errors: A problem for us all." *AAPOR News* 10:2, p. 1.

Rosenberg, Milton J., and Carl I. Hovland. 1960. "Cognitive, affective, and behavioral components of attitudes." In *Attitude Organization and Change*, by Milton J. Rosenberg, Carl I. Hovland, William J. McGuire, Robert P. Abelson, and Jack W. Brehm. New Haven, Ct., and London: Yale University Press.

Salmon, Charles T., and John Spicer Nichols. 1983. "The next-birthday method of respondent selection." *Public Opinion Quarterly* 47:270–276.

Sudman, Seymour. 1982. "The president and the polls." *Public Opinion Quarterly* 46:301–310.

Traugott, Michael W. 1985. "Respondent selection and pre-election estimates of candidate preference." Paper presented at May 1985 Conference of the American Association for Public Opinion Research.

———. 1987. "Persistence in respondent selection." *Public Opinion Quarterly* 51:48–57.

Traugott, Michael W., and Clyde Tucker. 1984. "Strategies for pre-

dicting whether a citizen will vote and estimation of electoral out-
comes.'' *Public Opinion Quarterly* 48:330–343.
Wolfinger, Raymond E., and Steven J. Rosenstone. 1980. *Who Votes?*
New Haven, Ct., and London: Yale University Press.

Index

A

ABC News/*Washington Post* Poll, 16, 60, 97, 104, 106, 137, 140, 143, 146
abortion issue, 42
academic: pollsters, 16; studies of voting behavior, 9, 91
accessibility, 43, 46–47
accuracy, 1–10; alternative measures of, 21–24; assessment of, 11, 12, 22–25, 25*n*; and call-backs, 45–46, 50; and candidate preference question position, 106–107; capabilities vs. limitations of, 11–12; and cluster sampling, 62; and commitment to candidate, 128; and conversion attempts, 47–49; and crystallization, 133; definition of, 21–22; and identification of likely voters, 74–76, 79–82, 93; importance of, 149–155, 164, 167, 172–173; and incumbency, 122–123; and interviewing facilities and staff, 159–161; in local elections, 125–127; and low information, 127; measuring, 17; methodological correlates of, 10, 11, 17; multivariate analysis of, 163–169; of national vs. state and local polls, 158; and nonsampling error, 171; and number of candidates, 103–104; and office at stake, 117–118; and party identification, 82–83; and political variables, 57–58; and poll analyst type, 155–158; and population interviewed, 38–39; and quotas, 27–29, 36, 46, 47; and random selection procedure, 50, 51, 52; and refusal rates, 47; and saliency, 127; and sample size, 63, 64–65; significance of, 6–7; and simulation of voting, 100; stratification and, 53, 54, 58; and telephone polls, 31, 47; and time pressures, 139; and timing of polling, 135–137; and turnout, 42, 68, 69, 94–95; and type of election, 131–132; and undecided vote, 109–110, 115; and weighting, 33–36; *see also* error
Adler, Kenneth, 8
affect, 6, 79, 86–87, 91, 118, 119, 120
age, 2, 38, 40, 41, 51, 52–53
Alderman, Jeffrey, 16, 77, 93, 104, 105, 106, 111, 143, 151
American Association for Public Opinion Research (AAPOR), 2, 9, 12
analysis plan, 23–24
anonymity, 47
antiabortion constituency, 94–95
a priori estimating model, 33
area codes, 54, 55
areal units, 58, 61
Arizona, 31, 70
attitudes, 6, 102, 182–183
"attract-attract" races, 120
available voting-age adult, 49, 50
awareness, 128

B

behavior: and attitude, 6; validation of, 91; *see also* voting behavior
Benson, Ed, 41
bias, 33, 145; and call-backs, 44, 50; and panels, 145
Black, Gordon, 3, 16, 31, 38, 42, 44, 47, 48, 52, 56, 63, 83, 87, 91, 106, 130, 137, 138, 144, 145
blacks, 31–32, 75, 86, 100; *see also* minorities; race
block clusters, 26
Bogart, Leo, 9
Bradley, Tom, 151

197

D1565913